A Brief Guide to Cipher Solving

By Megan Copley, Paul Fairhall, Jo Smedley

This book was brought to life thanks to donations from:

Erik Meijers
Dona Gray
Jennifer Mckenzie
Laura
Kathryn Baker
Danielle Ebany
Rogelio Lopez
Jodie Wong
Jodi
Minna Haatanen
Jennifer Medicus
Philip Harty
Kelly
Frankie Jasper
Karen Dudley
Sandra Varden
Rosie
.Tv.
Christie
Karin Olsson
Colin Thomson
Roxanne Miller
Lindsey Mull
Janell Julian
Anastazia
Robert
Elizabeth Winter
Charlie Wheeler
Stacy Monotrakis
David Bush
Jonathan Hebert
Rebecca
Alexander
Katy Bennett
Cammie Hall
Mindtroverted
Habibah
Becky Pearson
Ctnelson
Colin Bruce
Paul Munday
Liz Janson
Penny Vinik
Shrenik
Adrian Stein
Julie Reiser
Jason Petit
Mike Wilson
Thedoc318
Atron Seige
Matt Hargett
Steven Sweeney
Angela Leonard
Adrienne
Hajo
Darren Currie
Dave
Crystal Fleming
Nathan Dunbar
Jesse Williams
Carsten
Diane Hall
Eric Mcafee
Sanne Kassenberg
Tim S. Macneil
Laura Hatch
Davide
Nathan
Laura Richardson-Cheater
Gary Duke
Robert Gallerani
Neon
Stewart Andrew
Glenn Phillips
Emily Rochon
Emma Marshall
Marvin
Amy
Joe Young Iv
Microbe999
Daniel Alexander Kolb
Cinder Nickleson
Kali Sardina
Litlbeth
Krys And Chris
Familie Selman
Noah Waldner
Walter Thomas
Kzen
Fatih Yalcin
Burke Morton
Eric J. Francois
Woody Lai
Kevin Khoo
S K
Pjetko
Julie Christensen
Abraham Riggin
Rachael
Carrez_N
Pfefferkorn Shari
Kyle Wagner
Emily Rousell
Gordian Loomans
Ashleigh
Ken Vanden Branden
Jenna
Jess J Patton
Taryn Johnson
Gina Ahn
Alan Litteneker
Penguinonstrike
Phillip Humphreys
Alecia

Thank you!!

If you are an avid puzzle solver, you may find https://www.dcode.fr is a massive help to you. It is a website that has most of the regular codes and decoding tools available at the touch of a button!

Contents

Introduction

We see codes and ciphers every day and don't even notice they are there. Braille, Sign Language and Moon are three codes we are so familiar with that we never stop to think about them as a means of secret message transmission. However, if you don't know the language, all three provide a means of two people communicating without anyone else understanding what is being said.

We also deal with pictogram language every day and again, are so familiar with the concept that we don't stop to think that the message being communicated has been done so in code. The skull and crossbones symbolise poison or pirates depending on the context. If we see a radiation symbol on a door, we know not to go inside unprotected. Even traffic signals provide us with hidden messages; we cannot park there, we must stop at a red traffic light. If you haven't learned the traffic laws, you wouldn't understand the message being provided.

All language itself is a form of code. We all learn a foreign language in school, and without the correct information, we wouldn't be able to translate what is being said. Some languages use the same alphabet as ours, others use a slightly different one. Some languages read left to right, others right to left. Others, such as Chinese, are constructed of logographs, representing meanings rather than sounds.

When it comes to decoding a message, you must find out first what language the message is transmitted in. Spotting phrases, sequences or letter combinations is only possible if you know the language the information is written in to begin with. As you might imagine, this means many codebreaking institutions not only employ codebreakers, but also linguists who are able to fluently read a variety of different languages.

Why not take a walk around your local area, your place of work, or some local facilities and see how many coded messages you can spot. There will be far more than you think, all of which are telling you something that you have come to understand through rote learning. An alien arriving on our planet would find many of these messages indecipherable at first and would need to employ code breaking techniques to solve them.

Understanding what a message may be about often helps with codebreaking. Many wartime codes have been cracked thanks to early morning weather reports. Knowing the weather that day, allowed educated guesses as to what the message was likely to say and therefore allowed for swifter decoding.

This isn't unexpected. We use context all the time to understand interrupted calls or conversation. In a crowded or noisy room if you haven't heard what someone said properly, you make an educated guess based on context to fill in the gaps you missed. Codebreaking is similar. Knowing the context allows us to "fill in the gaps".

However, just decoding a message doesn't necessarily mean you understand it. The message could be complicated with code words or phrases. Codebreaking is only truly finished when you understand the message being sent, rather than just being able to read it.

A Brief History of Codes

When are codes and ciphers used?

People have been using codes and ciphers for thousands of years to send secret messages back and forth. Codes have evolved throughout time from simple codes and ciphers to the much more complex encryption codes used by computers today to send things electronically.

Humans have tried to conceal information in the written form since people began writing. Examples of secret messages still exist in stone inscriptions, papyrus and cuneiform tablets, indicating that the ancient Egyptians, Hebrews, and Babylonians all developed cryptographic systems to hide information.

One of the first known uses of cryptography came in the form of a cipher device known as a scytale. Scytales were used for secret communication between military commanders and consisted of a tapered baton with a strip of parchment or leather spirally wrapped around it. When wrapped, a message was then written on this strip. Once unwrapped the letters were scrambled, thus creating the cipher. When the strip was wrapped around a baton with the same proportions as the original, the message was revealed.

Julius Caesar was known to send secret messages to his army generals using the Caesar cipher. A form of substitution cipher, each character of the original text is substituted by another character to form the ciphertext. Caesar used the variant 'shift by three', which meant every character in his messages was shifted by three places. 'A' was replaced by 'D', 'B' was replaced by 'E' and so on.

Simple substitution ciphers depend on both the sender and the receiver being the only ones who know what the shift is or know what symbols have replaced what characters. They are easy to construct, but they are also often very easy to decode -

even if you aren't in possession of the original coding rules.

It is not common knowledge, but during the imprisonment of Mary Queen of Scots (in which she was not allowed contact with the outside world), she managed to smuggle letters in and out of the castle. Mary was helped by Gilbert Gifford, who was one of the few people she was allowed to see. Mary's codes included a homophonic substitution for letters, a homophonic substitution table for common letter combinations, and a list of code symbols for common words and expressions like "The Pope" and "Madame". She also had symbols for months of the year and currency. Mary used the cipher language she had created as part of a plot to assassinate Queen Elizabeth I. Unfortunately for her, Gifford was a double agent working for Queen Elizabeth's spymaster, Sir Francis Walsingham. He hired intelligence workers to decipher and read Mary's letters as soon as they were sent and received.

Cryptography has developed in complexity over time. Once a code is broken, a new code is required to keep messages hidden from the enemy. As an enemy creates a new coding system, another decoding system is developed to help break the code and read the encrypted messages.

In the early history of the United States, one-time cipher pads were widely used. During the American Civil War, the Confederate Army primarily used Vigenère ciphers and sometimes letter substitution. And during the First World War, the use of ciphers remained popular for protecting diplomatic communications.

By the 1920s there had been a revolution in communications as telegraphy, radio and the advances in electronic technology meant messages could be sent via signal.

The technological revolution also created a major advance in cryptography – the development of rotor cipher machines. Though the concept of a rotor had been used before with cipher wheels, Edward Hebern created a new, more complex rotary cipher machine.

The Hebern Rotor Machine looked like a small typewriter; it had 26 letters that lit up and a rotor on the top that scrambled the electrical signals between the letters of the keyboard and the light panel. When each letter was typed, the rotor rotated one space and gave a new scrambling sequence. This was a relatively weak cipher, but it inspired many other machines that worked with a similar rotor system. One of the most notable of these was the Enigma machine.

The Enigma machine was invented by German engineer Arthur Scherbius and proved almost impossible to break. Three Polish mathematicians were tasked with cracking the code and they began their work in the 1920s after the German navy began transmitting baffling messages.

They managed to break some of the Enigma messages, however it was not long before the Germans began changing the settings of the machine every day and Polish resources could no longer keep up. In July 1939, their work was handed over to codebreakers at Bletchley Park.

Though Enigma had some weaknesses, it was mainly thanks to human error that any successes in decoding the messages were achieved. German procedural flaws, operational mistakes and the failure to make systematic changes in coding procedures permitted some early decoding successes, but it was the capture of key tables and hardware that eventually enabled Allied cryptologists to succeed.

Breaking the Enigma code was one of the most important intelligence operations of the Second World War. The code was so difficult to break that traditional manual techniques could not decode it in time. It was so hard to break, in fact, that it required the invention of a computer. With the electronic assistance in place, the Allies broke their first encrypted message in January 1940.

Once the code was broken, ensuring that the German military didn't discover the Allies had broken the code and change it again became paramount. That particular secret was kept not just during the war, but for another 30 years!

These days, modern computers dominate the world of cryptology. Most of the world is digitally connected, and scientists and hackers have discovered they can use malware (malicious software) to steal, exploit and destroy data from digital devices that completely evades their in-built protection with cryptography. Although quantum computing makes cryptography potentially even more difficult to decipher, the codes used remain breakable. The only problem is that it takes a huge amount of time to break them, even with the speed of our modern-day computers. By the time a code is broken the message it is often no longer relevant, or the code has been replaced by a newer more secure system.

Well-known code users

Samuel Pepys

Samuel Pepys was a prominent member of society in Restoration London and he kept personal diaries until 1669. Pepys' diaries contained not only very personal accounts but also notes on political events, gossip and major crises such as the Great Fire of London and the plague.

His entries began on New Year's Day in 1660 and he wrote using a form of shorthand developed by Thomas Shelton. At first glance, the diary looked like random dots and squiggles, with only one or two of the words recognizable to the untrained eye. We now know a lot more about Samuel Pepys, and it is thought that he wrote in this way to hide information about the extra-marital affairs he is known to have had!

George Washington and the Culper Spy Ring

During the revolutionary war, both the British and American forces employed networks of spies to gain critical information about the war efforts of the other side. In November 1778, George Washington appointed Major Benjamin Tallmadge as director of military intelligence. It was his job to create a spy ring in New York City where the British headquarters were located.

Tallmadge used several protective measures to keep the identities of his spies secret. One of these came in the form of a numerical substitution system to identify informants, rather than the use of names. Some 763 numbers were used, with 745 representing 'England', 711, 'General Washington', and 727 'New York' and all spies were given pseudonyms.

The network of spies became known as the Culper Spy Ring and was made up Tallmadge's school friends; Abraham Woodhull, Anna Strong, Austin Roe and Caleb Brewster, who worked together to collect and re-distribute information about enemy movements. For five years they operated successfully in and around New York without being detected by the British, even though they had to pass through British held territory in order to pass on their secret messages.

Beatrix Potter

When she was around fourteen years old Beatrix Potter began to keep a coded journal, taking inspiration from James Boswell and Samuel Pepys, who had famously kept diaries themselves. Potter was quite restricted in her life and was expected to be a quiet, obedient daughter, so her journal was a place for her to escape. In her diary, Potter spoke of subjects such as Shakespeare and political events and critiqued artists such as Michelangelo, saying his work was 'hideous and badly drawn'.

Though not keeping the type of secrets that would help win wars or overthrow the monarchy, keeping a coded journal allowed Potter to have control over something and express herself more freely than she otherwise could.

JRR Tolkien

A step beyond creating codes, is the decision to construct an entirely new, previously unknown language from scratch. This is what JRR Tolkien did during his writing career. The most developed languages he constructed featured in his tales of middle earth, namely Quenya and Sindarin. Both were designed from phonesthetic considerations and Quenya in particular was based on Latin, with elements from other languages like Finnish, Welsh, English and Greek.

Lost languages

Languages don't last forever. Like the people who create them, they are alive for only as long as the people who use them. Languages die gradually over time as other languages take over and become more dominant. There are many indigenous languages the world over that are gradually falling out of use. When this happens, the decoding of what one person was saying to another often becomes very difficult. It will require an understanding of how the language was formed, the culture surrounding the language and how the written word was constructed.

In some cases, direct action has helped to revive old languages. This is particularly true of Welsh, where today around 30% of the people of Wales can speak it and many more understand it.

However, over our history as the human race, we have gradually lost the ability to read and write in a variety of languages. These languages are now only possible to read thanks to the work of archaeological codebreakers, who have spent years studying lost languages to try and decipher what the ancient people were communicating to each other. Work on many languages is still ongoing in different parts of the world, and even now there are at least twelve lost languages still waiting to be deciphered by archaeologists.

Sometimes what is needed is a lucky break; perhaps a familiar word or a context that makes a translation possible. This was just what happened with the team trying to decode hieroglyphics when the Rosetta Stone was discovered in 1799.

The Rosetta Stone was unique in the ancient world and it was key in the understanding of Egyptian hieroglyphics. Carved into granite, it contained three identical texts of a royal decree written in Hieroglyphics, Demotic and Ancient Greek.

With Ancient Greek already known and understood in the

scientific community, the Rosetta Stone became an ancient codex and provided a means for scholars to decode the other two scripts.

Thomas Young, an English physicist, was one of the first to recognize that some of the hieroglyphs written on the Rosetta Stone spelled out the sounds of a royal name: Ptolemy.

Following this initial breakthrough, Jean-François Champollion, a French scholar, postulated that hieroglyphs recorded the sound of the Egyptian language and in 1822 he declared that he had translated the entire text.

These days hieroglyphics are never used correctly in modern puzzle books and games. Instead, when you find the symbols, you are more likely to be looking at a direct letter substitution code. This is because most people can't speak ancient Egyptian!

Other ancient languages are also often misused in this way. Runes are regularly used in puzzle stories, but again, like hieroglyphs are often used as a letter substitution rather than to create actual Norse words.

Secret Words and Secret Messages...

There are a variety of ways you can hide messages within what appears to be plain English without using letter substitution, ciphers or codes.

Acrostic poems are the most common example of this, where the first letter of each line creates a word.

Other times the message is conveyed by a change in the formatting of letters or their position e.g. using just the first letter of the first word in every sentence, or every first letter in a sentence, only the letters in capitals, or the letters in bold, or the letters underlined like in the example below.

> **Encoded message:**
>
> *Hello! Everything is looking great. Lots of things still to finish. Please see my email for a list of tasks still to complete. Maybe you can delegate something to Tim? Everything looks on track to be finished on time.*

Here are some for simple examples for you to look at.

A letter home to a friend:

Are you able to send over maps of the region? I'm eager to visit
but I'd like to have an idea of the lay of the land first.
Charlotte says there are wonderful museums. I'd love to hear
your opinion on the best ones.
Recently, I've found that I go to places and become incredibly
bored as I already know the info.
Of course, there is always a chance I'll learn something new,

but my eagerness has depleted somewhat.
Something new must be out there though – and if anyone knows where, it's you, I'm sure!
Tell Paul I miss him and the kids. I bet they've gotten big since I last saw them. How time flies.
I'll have to tell Charlotte that seeing you is one of our priorities on this break, as well as exploring.
Catch you soon. Until then, goodbye.

Sightseeing in Cambridge:

The Cambrid**g**e University Bot**a**nic Ga**r**den lies between Trumpington Roa**d** and Bat**e**man Street and covers a**n** area of 16 hectares. To visit the gardens, ticket**s** must be purchased in advance. Those who have visited st**a**te that the ga**r**den is nice and peaceful and that the various wat**e**r features and raise**d** walkway cr**e**ate a relaxing atmosphere. It has been dubbed a 'perfe**c**t escap**e** from the city **n**oise and smoky air', a s**t**atement I believe **t**o be accurate.

When it comes to adding codes, these can sometimes be hidden in plain sight, like morse code or braille in a border graphic. Once you start looking for them, it's very hard to stop. And you begin to see patterns everywhere, even when there aren't any!

Some hidden messages can be revealed only by combining two or more sheets to read a message which is split between two or three pieces of paper, or only revealed when you fold the paper in a certain way.

Cardan Grille

Gerolamo Cardon, a Renaissance mathematician, is said to have created the Cardan Grille in 1550. Cardan grilles are made from sheets of paper, parchment, or very thin metal which is ruled to represent lines of handwriting. Cardan grilles have rectangular cutouts, so when an encoder places the grille on a piece of paper, they can write their messages into these gaps. These gaps may allow room for letters, syllables or even whole words.

Once the grille has been removed from the sheet of paper, the encoder fills in the rest of the text, creating a note or letter which disguises their true message.

The recipient of messages encoded using a Cardan grille must possess an identical grille. Grilles can be placed in four positions; face up, face down, upright and reversed, thus increasing the number of possible positions.

In practice, it can be difficult to use Cardan grilles as they can lead to stilted language and the physical grilles are subject to being lost or stolen.

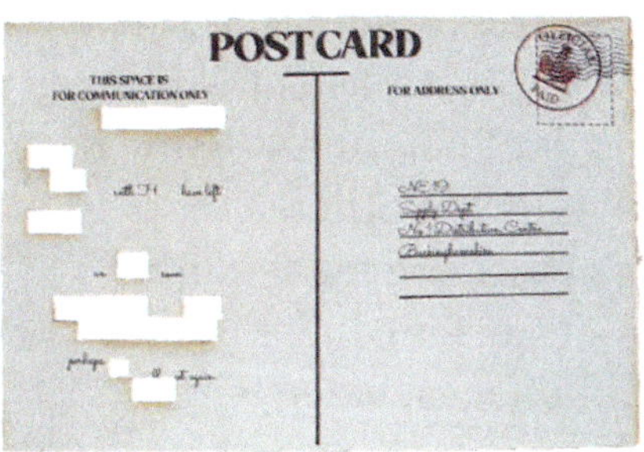

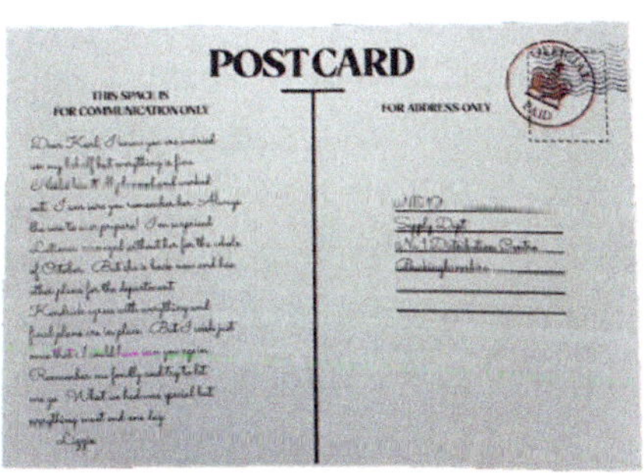

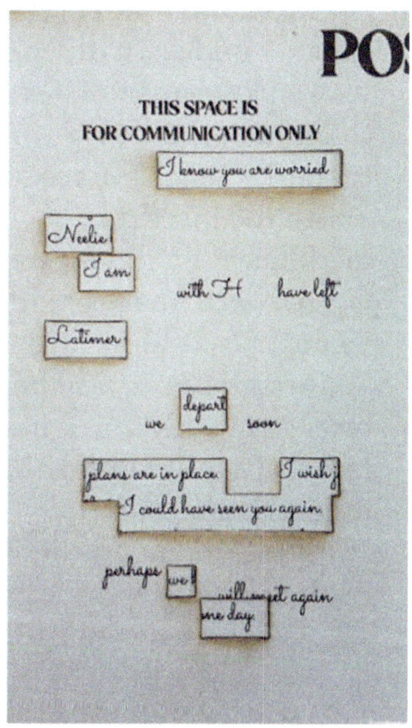

Steganography

Steganography is the practice of hiding a message within a visible non-secret message.

The word itself is derived from the Greek word *steganos* meaning hidden, and the Greek word *graph* meaning to write.

Steganography has an advantage over cryptography, because plainly visible encrypted messages, no matter how unbreakable they are, arouse interest and may in itself be incriminating in countries in which encryption is illegal such as Belarus, Kazakhstan, Mongolia, Pakistan, Singapore, Tunisia and Vietnam.

Steganography can take many forms. Some you may already have tried at home; e.g. writing the message in lemon juice, clear wax, invisible ink, or heat changing ink so that the message is only visible when you treat the paper it is written on.

Different coloured overlays can be used to hide and reveal messages, these work in a similar way to the colour-blindness tests you might have seen where those who are red/green colour-blind see a different number to everyone else.

A well known audio version of steganography is the morse code that is hidden within Barrington Pheloung's theme tune to the TV series, Morse. You may know of others.

With the invention of computers there are many digital methods of hiding messages. Data transfer can be multi-layered with images hidden within images, video within video, or by adding layers to audio.

Information can also be concealed as microdots, which are texts or images which have been reduced to a very small size (around a millimetre) and then hidden within a seemingly innocent document.

This technique was developed during World War 2 by Professor Zapp as a means of transmitting secret information. They were used extensively by all parties, especially the

French and Germans. Spies would photograph secret messages and reduce their size to a dot, then insert it into another ordinary message. Upon receiving the message, the secret message would be extracted and enlarged again to become readable.

In modern digital steganography, data is first encrypted and then inserted by computer into a particular file format such as a JPEG image, audio file or video file. Different techniques exist to transmit messages in this way, and it requires both parties to be aware of the technique used in order to identify the files that contain these secret messages. Hidden messages are a regular trope in movies and TV shows, with computer experts finding hidden messages in files and images.

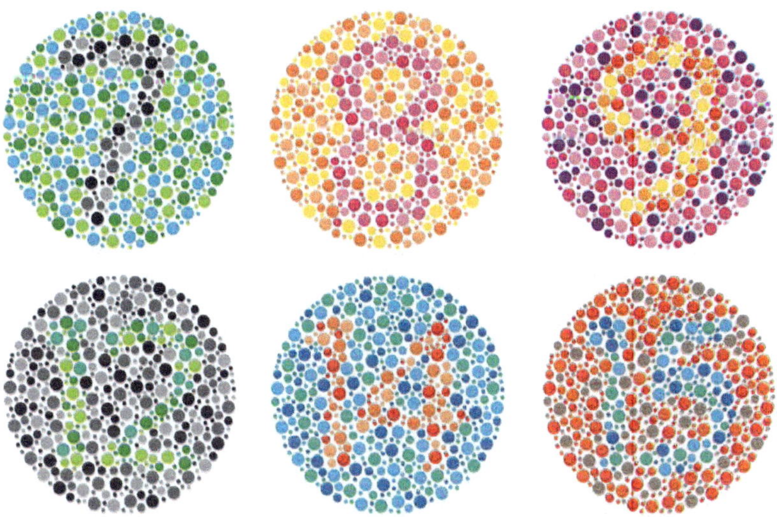

Scytale

Some of the earliest ciphers in recorded history are scytale ciphers. Scytales are the easiest way of creating a transpositional cipher and were likely originally written in plain text.

Scytale ciphers were first mentioned by the Greek poet Archilochus who lived in 7th century BC. It is likely they were in use some time before he wrote about them and they were still being used as late as AD 120 when they were described by Plutarch, a well known politician, priest and philosopher.

Scytale is the Greek word for baton which is how the message was encoded and decoded. Two commanders would have the same size rod created. Messages were written on leather or thick parchment that was wrapped in one long strip around the baton so that no wood was visible. Messages were written across the baton, unrolled and then sent to the other commander. On receipt of the message, the jumble of letters could only be read once it was wrapped around a similar sized baton.

Scytales are effectively the world's first column ciphers as they can be decoded in much the same way (column ciphers are discussed later). Once you know how many letters fit around the baton, you do not need the baton to be able to decode the message. You can simply rearrange the letters into columns according to the number of letters that fit around the rod.

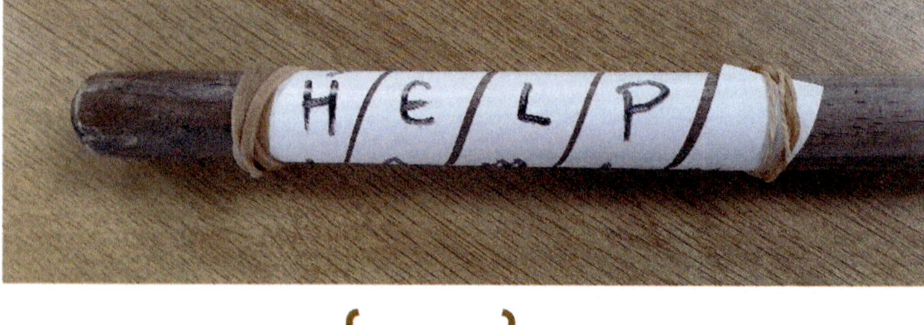

Directional Codes

Directional codes are some of the easiest codes to work with, but they can be difficult to get started!

These codes rely on you reading the text in a way that isn't the traditional left to right pattern.

The likelihood is you will have come across this style of code before, as this is how acrostic poetry is made. In acrostic poems, you read the letters downwards instead of the sentences across the page to spell out words.

Sometimes directional codes can be used in conjunction with another code. If you work out a letter substitution or other cipher and think it doesn't seem right, it may well be because it's also been encoded using a directional code too.

F	I	V	E	B
C	A	N	B	Y
S	E	R	E	F
D	P	U	S	I
I	R	G	E	V

Here's one for you to try...

T	H	P	U	E	M	T	E
E	E	Z	E	T	R	D	I
S	Z	S	O	E	I	H	L
L	S	G	H	O	W	E	R
E	E	T	U	A	B	A	E
T	A	S	R	U	E	S	O
R	A	E	T	M	T	L	K
F	T	S	O	I	L	A	Y

Helpful Alphabets

In this section we will look at different alphabets that are often used in letter substitutions. We will explore their origins, how they were used, and in some cases, why they were developed.

Semaphore

Semaphore is a method of visual signalling and was used to transmit messages between distant points from high towers before the invention of the telegraph.

It was also used to signal between ships and would be done by persons who held a small flag in each hand. They would change their hand positions to different angles to indicate different letters or numbers.

Air marshalling also uses a form of semaphore, as marshals direct aircraft into position at airports and on aircraft carriers. In this case, the hand positions represent actions rather than letters, such as 'all clear', 'cut engines', 'turn right', or 'insert chocks'. Helicopter marshalling is slightly different and includes other signals such as 'hold hover' and 'release sling load'.

As well as using flags, people can communicate with semaphore using a range of tools such as rods, paddles or just with their hands!

The current semaphore system uses two poles with square flags. They are also coloured differently, depending on whether the signals are sent by sea or by land. On land, semaphore flags are white and blue, while at sea they are red and yellow. Using these coloured flags helps make the letters more obvious from a distance. When you are proficient in Semaphore you can read and send messages quite fast!

Have a go at solving this message:

Morse Code

Morse code is a method used to encode text as sequences of dots and dashes and it can be transmitted in several ways, e.g. via sound waves or using flashing light. It can be directly interpreted by those with an understanding of Morse.

Morse code was initially developed by American artist Samuel Morse as a system of telegraphy. Before the telegraph was invented, messages to be sent over a long distance took a long time to send, but the telegraph allowed for fast transmission using electricity.

Telegraph messages were sent by tapping out code in the form of long and short signals. Short signals were represented as dots and long signals as dashes. The code formed by the dots and dashes was then sent over telegraph wires and converted into electrical impulses. On the other end of the wire, a telegraph receiver would convert the impulses back into dots and dashes so they could decode the message.

The most well-known Morse signal is the distress signal SOS, which in Morse looks like this:

... --- ...

Experienced Morse operators are able to send and receive messages at a rate of 20-30 words per minute. Morse was designed to keep codes as short as possible, meaning that the most common letters in the alphabet have shorter symbols. E, for example, has only one dot, N has only one dash and one dot, A has only one dot and a dash etc. as these are the most commonly used letters of the English language.

Morse code

A	• —	S	• • •
B	— • • •	T	—
C	— • — •	U	• • —
D	— • •	V	• • • —
E	•	W	• — —
F	• • — •	X	— • • —
G	— — •	Y	— • — —
H	• • • •	Z	— — • •
I	• •	1	• — — — —
J	• — — —	2	• • — — —
K	— • —	3	• • • — —
L	• — • •	4	• • • • —
M	— —	5	• • • • •
N	— •	6	— • • • •
O	— — —	7	— — • • •
P	• — — •	8	— — — • •
Q	— — • —	9	— — — — •
R	• — •	0	— — — — —

Try to decode these messages:

1) .. .-. .- - .... . .-. .-.. .. -.- . -.. --- .. -. --. -- --- .-. ... . -.-. --- -.. .

2) - .... . .-. . .- .-. . .---- ..--- -- --- -. - .... -. .- -.-- . .- .-.

Pigpen cipher

Pigpen is a form of substitution cipher in which the letters are replaced by symbols. Throughout history, the Pigpen cipher has been used by many groups, including an 18th century secret society known as the Freemasons.

It is not known where the cipher originated, though some believe it started with secret communications between Hebrew rabbis. There is also evidence that it was used during the Christian Crusades in the Middle Ages.

Pigpen Alphabet

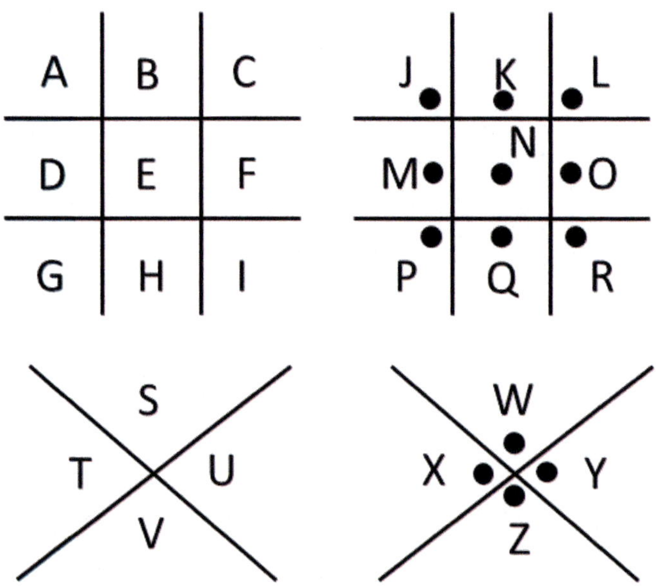

The letters are written as the lines and dots that surround them, so in the case above:

The letter A would be shown as 
The letter O would be shown as 
The letter X would be shown as 

It's worth noting, that Pigpen ciphers vary depending on how the letters are set up, but there are two common standard ones. Either the alphabet moves through the "squares", then the triangles, or it moves through all "non dotted" shapes, then all the dotted shapes. (Though there are some additional variations on which letters are located where from time to time).

Try to decode this message based on the example provided:
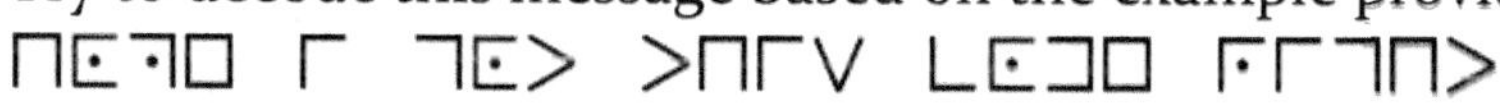

An alternative interpretation is below:

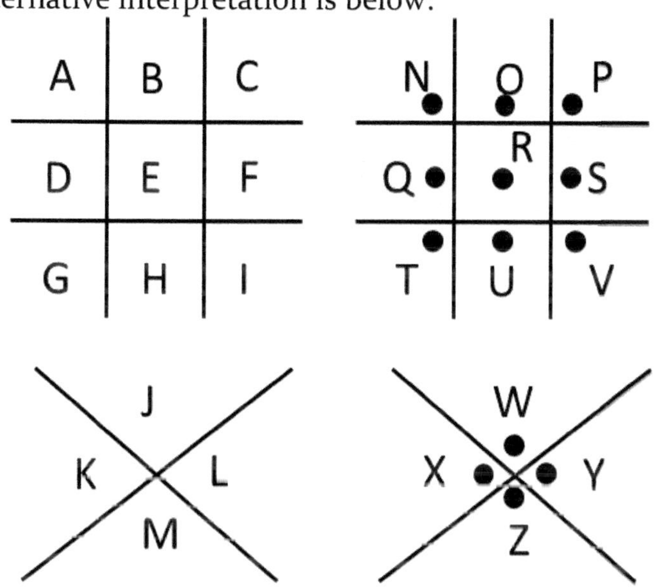

Templar Cipher

The Templar cipher is a variant of the Pigpen cipher, that uses a variant of the Maltese Cross to convert letters to symbols. The cross was the emblem of the Knights Hospitallers and Templars during the crusades.

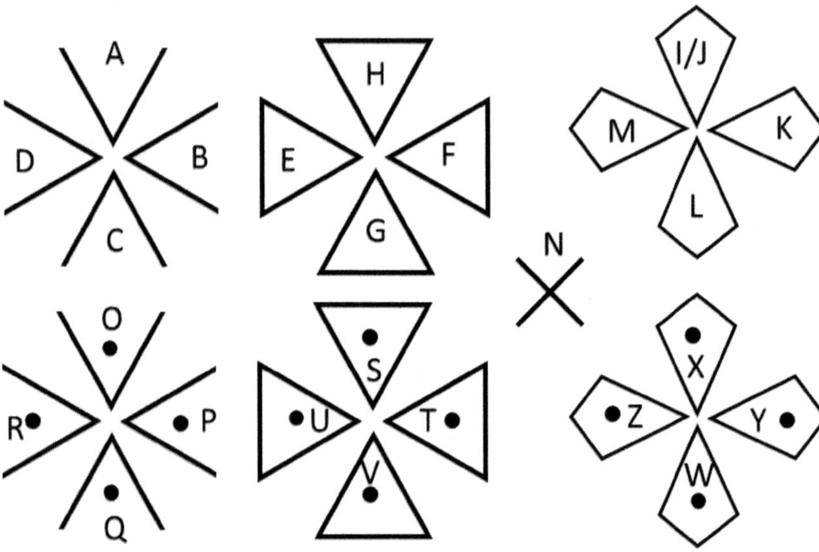

It is likely that this code was used by the Freemasons (or Neo-Templars) during the 18th century, rather than the religious order of the Knights Templar.

Once again, the letters are written as the lines and dots that surround them, so:

The letter A would be shown as 

The letter O would be shown as 

The letter X would be shown as 

Try decoding this one:

Atbash Cipher

The Atbash cipher is a monoalphabetic cipher that is formed by taking the alphabet and reversing it.

A	B	C	D	E	F	G	H	I	J	K	L	M
↕	↕	↕	↕	↕	↕	↕	↕	↕	↕	↕	↕	↕
Z	Y	X	W	V	U	T	S	R	Q	P	O	N

The first letter ‘A’ becomes the last letter ‘Z’, the second letter ‘B’, becomes ‘Y’ and so on.

The name Atbash derives from the first, second, last and second to last letters of the Hebrew alphabet, as this is the alphabet it was originally used to encrypt.

Atbash can be modified for use with any known writing system

See if you can decode the following message:

GSRH XLWV RH VZHB GL YIVZP

Dancing Men Cipher

The Dancing Men cipher originated in Sir Arthur Conan Doyle’s Sherlock Holmes story ‘The Adventure of the Dancing Men’, and is a simple letter substitution cipher. Sherlock deciphered the code by conducting frequency analysis, though even Conan Doyle made some errors with the transcription! Flags held by the figures symbolised the end of a word.

Try this one:

Caesar Cipher

Caesar ciphers are one of the earliest known and simplest ciphers. The Caesar cipher is called by this name as it was used by Julius Caesar and his generals to send secret messages to one another. Encoding his messages in this way meant that his enemies could not read them, and therefore his military tactics and other confidential information could not be leaked.

Caesar ciphers can be shifted by any number of letters, and sometimes codes using this method will include a key. This type of cipher is very common, and it is probably one of the first ciphers you will have encountered as it is often used as an educational tool to teach problem-solving.

A Caesar cipher is a type of letter substitution cipher in which each letter in the message is 'shifted' a certain number of places down the alphabet. For example, if you used A+1, then the letter A would be replaced by the letter B, the the letter B would become C, C would become D and so on.

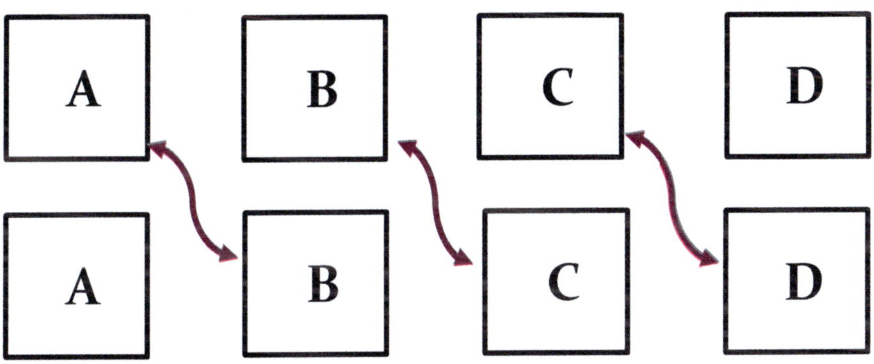

Due to the simplicity of Caesar ciphers, they are often used in conjunction with other ciphers or languages just to make them more complex to solve.

Caesar ciphers can be harder to solve when a language with shared lettering is used as the base language, e.g. Egyptian hieroglyphs, where letters can share a symbol.

How do you make a Caesar Cipher?

When making a Caesar cipher, knowing what you want your code to say is a good starting place! As an example, we'll use the phrase, "I really hate Morse code", but to make it trickier, we're going to write it in Morse too!

.. / .-. . .- .-.. .-.. -.-- / .... .- - . / -- --- .-. ... . / -.-. --- -.. .

Now we have the original Morse message, we're going to shift it by three. This will give us:

L UHDOOB KDXH PRUVH FRGH

Or in Morse...

.-.. / ..- .... -.. --- --- -... / -.- -.. -..- .... / .--. .-. ..- ...- .... / ..-. .-. --. ....

Here are some for you to try...

Let's start with an easy one.

1) M eq kixxmrk xli lerk sj xlmw (C4)

Now we'll look at some trickier ones.

2) .--. .-. ..- ...- .... / ..-. .-. --. .... / .-.. ...- / --.- .-. .-- / .-- -.- -.. .-- / -.- -.. ..- --. / ..- .... -.. --- --- -... (C3)

3) 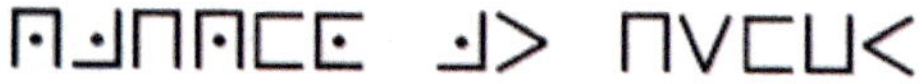 (C1)

Bacon Cipher

The Bacon cipher uses a bilateral substitution alphabet, usually made up of the letters 'A' and 'B'. This cipher was invented by Francis Bacon in 1605 purely because he loved to write using secret messages.

One example of a Bacon alphabet is shown below:

A = AAAAA	B = AAAAB	C = AAABA
D = AAABB	E = AABAA	F = AABAB
G = AABBA	H = AABBB	I/J = ABAAA
K = ABAAB	L = ABABA	M = ABABB
N = ABBAA	O = ABBAB	P = ABBBA
Q = ABBBB	R = BAAAA	S = BAAAB
T = BAABA	U/V = BAABB	W = BABAA
X = BABAB	Y = BABBA	Z = BABBB

Decoding these messages looks hard because of the sheer number of letters involved, but actually it's just another form of letter substitution cipher. All you need to do is recognise the combinations as individual letters.

Bacon ciphers can also be coded in another way, taking a code and concealing it in a sentence five times its length, allowing messages to be hidden within a larger section of text which makes it harder to detect and decipher.

"Midnight" for example could be sent as, "sIr FRaNcis bacON wAs aLiVe in fiFTeen SIXTy-tWo".

Note how in the sentence, certain characters are capitalised whilst some are not? The capitalised letters here represent the 'B's of the Bacon cipher, and the lower case letters the 'A's.

sIr FRaNcIs bacON wAs aLiVe in fiFTeen SIXTy- tWo
ABABB ABAAA AAABB ABAAB ABAAA AABBA AABBB BAABA

By breaking the As and Bs into five-letter groups (ABABB/ABAAA etc), you can now read the coded message, which in this case is 'midnight'.

Here's one for you to try:

4) BAABA AABBB AABAA BAAAB AABAA AAABA ABAAA ABBBA AABBB AABAA BAAAA BAAAB AAAAA BAAAA AABAA ABABB AAAAA ABAAB ABAAA ABBAA AABBA ABABB AABAA AABBB BAABB ABBAA AABBA BAAAA BABBA

Breaking Letter Substitution Codes

A letter substitution cipher replaces the letters in the alphabet with symbols or another random letter.

An example of a letter substitution cipher can be seen below.

MKF WMKFY CZG E UZP PZM UEMK LG UERF ZVC PKF ZPTFC LLF MW NZPP KFY MKF SENPMEAT ZVC E ZAAECFVMZSSG NZPPFC KFY Z XSHF PMEAT.

PKF PMESS EPVM MZSTEVX MW LF.

To solve the cipher you need to know first the language it is written in, and ideally be fluent in that language and understand the basic rules which that language follows.

This message was written in English. There are four basic facts about the English language that will help us considerably when solving a cipher.

1) The most common letter in the English language is E, followed by A, R, I, O, T, N and S.
2) The most common three-letter words are AND and THE.
3) Single letters are usually the words A or I
4) The most frequent double-letter combinations are ee, ll, ss, oo, tt,ff, rr, nn, pp, and cc. The double letters that occur most commonly at the end of words are ee, ll, ss, and ff.

So the first step in the solving process is to look at the cipher and identify where we can apply these rules.

The quickest method is often to look for the most common letter.

F is the most common cipher letter in this paragraph, so initially we'll presume that F is the letter E. Sometimes the most common letter isn't E, in which case you may want to try some of the other common letters until you find the right substitution that creates a pattern that appears to be consistent with what we know about the English language.

Changing our F's to E's gives us the following:

MKe WMKeY CZG E UZP PZM UUEMK LG UERe ZVC PKe ZPTeC Le MW NZPP KeY MKe SENPMEAT ZVC E ZAAECeVMZSSG NZPPeC KeY Z XSHe PMEAT.
PKe PMESS EPVM MZSTEVX MW Le.

Knowing the e, we can easily spot some three letter word combinations that are most likely to be THE.
MKe is repeated twice in this paragraph and so is ZVC.

MKe WMKeY CZG E UZP PZM UUEMK LG UERe ZVC PKe ZPTeC Le MW NZPP KeY MKe SENPMEAT ZVC E ZAAECeVMZSSG NZPPeC KeY Z XSHe PMEAT.
PKe PMESS EPVM MZSTEVX MW Le.

From this, we can guess that the MKe one is 'the' (it is more common for sentences and paragraphs to begin with "the" than "and"), and we could also try replacing ZVC with the word 'and'.

The WMKeY CZG E UZP PZM UUEMK LG UERe and PKe ZPTeC Le MW NZPP KeY the SENPMEAT and E ZAAECeVMZSSG NZPPeC KeY Z XSHe PMEAT.
PKe PMESS EPVM MZSTEVX MW Le.

We can now fill in the newly discovered letters and replace all the Zs, Vs and C's with As, Ns and D's (as per our guess that ZVC is the word 'AND'), and replace all the Ms and K's with T's and H's (as per our guess that MKF is the word 'the').

The WtheY daG E UaP Pat UEth LG UERe and Phe aPTed Le tW NaPP heY the SENPtEAT and E aAAEdentaSSG NaPPed heY a

XSHe PtEAT.
Phe PtESS EPnt taSTEnX tW Le.

As you can see this is starting to look a lot like English.

Now it's important to try making some further assumptions - the easiest one to guess is the cipher letter that is on its own - E.

We can rule out A on the basis that it has already been used in the word AND, so E must be the letter I.

We can also see two 3-letter words ending in 'he'. These are most likely to be 'the' or 'she' and as we've used 'the' earlier, we can assume it's 'she'.

In addition to this, we have a 2-letter word beginning with 't' - that can **only** be 'to'.

The WtheY daG E UaP Pat UEth LG UERe and Phe aPTed Le tW NaPP heY the SENPtEAT and E aAAEdentaSSG NaPPed heY a XSHe PtEAT.
Phe PtESS EPnt taSTEnX tW Le.

Now let's go through the cipher replacing the letters with the newly found ones, as below...

The otheY daG I Uas sat Uith LG UiRe and she asTed Le to Nass heY the SiNstiAT and I aAAidentaSSG Nassed heY a XSHe stiAT.
She stiSS isnt taSTinX to Le.

Next we need to focus on certain letters which look easy to solve:

The 5 letter word starting with 'sti' and with two of the same letter at the end of the word – can only be "stiff" or "still"

The 4 letter words ending with ith – can only be "pith" or "with"

The 5 letter word starting othe – can only be "other"

The 3 letter words staring with 'da' – can only be "day", "dab" or "dam"

Now our cipher is coming together nicely, and we currently have the following:

The other day I was sat with Ly wiRe and she asTed Le to Nass her the liNsticT and I accidentally Nassed her a XlHe sticT.

She still isn't talTinX to Le.

We can now guess the sentence based on the context, and fill in more of the letters:

The other day I was sat with my wife and she asked me to pass her the lipstick and I accidentally passed her a glue stick.

She still isn't talking to me.

This makes the cipher:

A	B	C	D	E	F	G	H	I	J	K	L	M
Z	L	A	X	F	R	*	K	E	*	T	S	L

N	O	P	Q	R	S	T	U	V	W	X	Y	Z
V	W	N	*	Y	P	M	H	*	U	*	G	*

Notice how we still don't know how some of the letters are encoded. This is because these letters were not needed in the original coded note. As such, we don't need to worry about them in this instance.

As with all decoding work, the more you practise the quicker you become. So here are some more secret messages for you to decipher in the same way as the previous anecdote:

1) RMI EPQIZINI CPGMIN JKT PZEIZRIF PZ SPSRIIZ SPSRL RMNII KZF XTIF RU VI OZUJZ KT RMI XZVNIKOKVAI CPGMIN.

2) G KUIW UTLUQY LUMPWZ PE CE PE FWVB UMZ YWW JUAKB FGAAKB. PKWVW UVW EIWV EMW KBMZVWZ XTGCKPY EX YPUGVY. G RWP GP'Y WNKUBYPGMC.

This next one is a little trickier as every letter pair equates to just one letter, like in a knock code which you'll learn more about shortly.

3) ITGT IRBEGTGA BC NCITGTGTNCBE GTGRITBAIEITBEGR ORIABENA GTORNT NCBEGTGTBEGRGA BCGRBE GEGABEBT GTNT GRBENEGRBEGABENAGT NTNABE GAGTNTNE ORBE IANTNEBE GTIAITGA IENANTBAIE BANTBTBE IABCGA NANTGT BRBEBENA GTNTNT BTITICICITBAGENCGT

Knock Codes

Knock code, or tap code, is based on the Polybius square, which is a 5x5 grid with 26 letters placed into 25 cells. It is called a knock or tap code because messages are transmitted using a series of tap or knocking sounds. Prisoners have been known to communicate with each other in this manner, tapping on the metal bars or walls of their cells. This method of communication was particularly prevalent during the Vietnam War, where isolated prisoners would use tap code to communicate between cells, telling each other what questions to expect during interrogations, if anyone was injured or in need of extra rations.

	1	2	3	4	5
1	A	B	C	D	E
2	F	G	H	I/J	K
3	L	M	N	O	P
4	Q	R	S	T	U
5	V	W	X	Y	Z

Using the square above the word "Help" would be "2,3 1,5 3,1 3,5" or, written into dots (symbolising each tap):

.. ... / . ..... / ... . / ... .

Knock codes can use five letter replacements instead of numbers. Because a maximum of 10 letters or numbers are used in combination to make up the code, it makes them quite easy to spot. If you find a message using just 10 letters, the chances are it's a knock code cipher created using a Polybius square.

An example of a letter encoded 5x5 square can be seen here:

	F	**R**	**U**	**I**	**T**
M	A	B	C	D	E
A	F	G	H	I/J	K
N	L	M	N	O	P
G	Q	R	S	T	U
O	V	W	X	Y	Z

The above square has been created using the words Mango and Fruit. To code a message using this square, you would replace the letter you want within the grid with the pair of letters on the XY axis. If you wanted to encode the letter A, your code would be MF. If you wanted to encode the letter S, your letter pair would be GU. Decoding would be the same process in reverse.

Knock codes can be decoded without knowing the placement of the letters within the square using simple letter substitution decoding techniques.

Using the square above, make up a code for the following messages:

1) THE DOG HAS BITTEN THE OLD WOMAN
2) -.. --- -. --- - .- ... -.- -- . .-- .... -.--

Playfair Cipher

The Playfair cipher was the first cipher in cryptologic history to encrypt pairs of letters. The cipher was invented by Charles Wheatstone in 1854 and due to it encrypting pairs, it was significantly harder to break through frequency analysis than simple substitution ciphers.

When it was first developed, use of the Playfair cipher was rejected by the British Foreign Office as they thought it would be too complicated to use. However British forces made use of the cipher on several occasions during the Second Boer War, World War I and even in World War II.

The Playfair cipher uses a 5x5 table containing a key word. To create the table, the first spaces in the table are filled with the letters of the keywords, and the rest of the letters of the alphabet in order. If, for example, you used the keyword "QUAIL", the key square would look like this:

Q	U	A	I/J	L
B	C	D	E	F
G	H	K	M	N
O	P	R	S	T
V	W	X	Y	Z

To encrypt a message, it first needs to be broken down into bigrams. For example, the message "Fly me to the moon" would become “FL YM ET OT HE MO ON”. If the message ends in an odd letter, the usual practice is to add an ‘X’ to make a pair.

There are several rules that need to be considered when forming encryption using this grid that are all based on the shape formed by the pairs of letters.

F and L are on the same column. If the letters are in the same column then they are transposed down one row, meaning that ‘F’ would become ‘N’ and ‘L’ would become ‘F’, so FL becomes NF. (If the letter was a Z, the you would wrap to the top, so Z would become I.)

Q	U	A	I/J	L
B	C	D	E	F
G	H	K	M	N
O	P	R	S	T
V	W	X	Y	Z

YM would be encrypted the same way, so YM becomes IS.

ET is next to be encrypted and as they are on different rows and columns, a different rule needs applying. In this case a rectangle is formed and the letters are swapped to the letter in the same row as them but at the opposite corner. ‘E’ becomes ‘F’ and ‘T’ becomes ‘S’ - ET becomes FS.

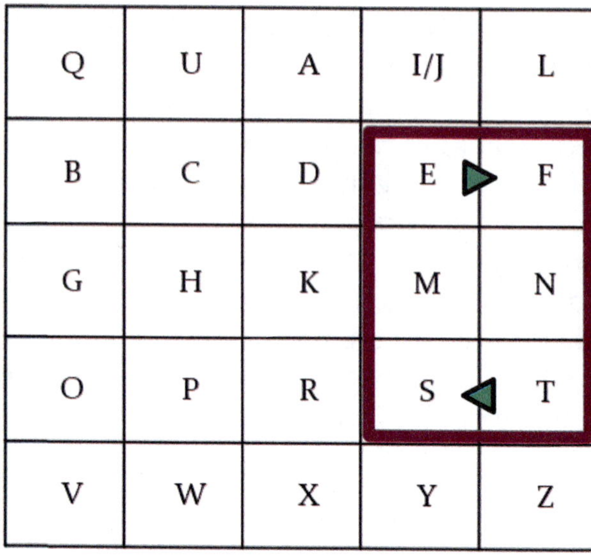

This "corner rule" means even if there are letters in between the pairs – only the corner letters are used.

With the next pair, we will be using another new rule. As O and T fall on the same row, they become the letters to their right. 'O' becomes 'P', and 'T' becomes 'O'. OT becomes PO.

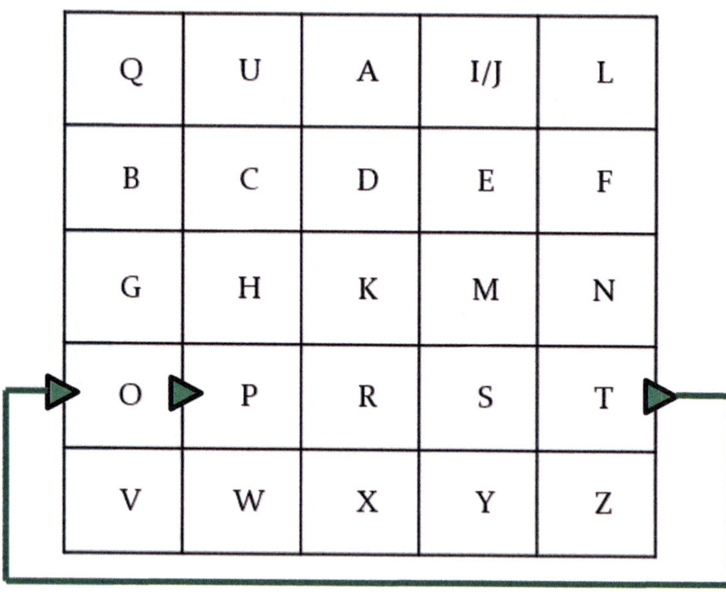

Now we know all of the rules, we can encrypt the rest. HE becomes MC, MO becomes GS and ON becomes TG.

Our new message is, therefore:

"NFISFSPOMCGSTG"

There is one more rule that doesn't apply with the above cipher. If both letters are the same (for instance 'EE'), you need to put an 'X' after the first letter. In the phrase 'STEEP HILL', the bigram would become ST/EX/EP/HI/LX/LX.

There are quite a few rules to remember with this cipher!

Using the above keyword of 'QUAIL', see how you get on with coding the following message:

I WILL NEED TO KEEP MY WITS ABOUT ME

Vigenère Ciphers

A Vigenère cipher is a form of letter substitution cipher that is incredibly difficult to break. It operates by changing the cipher shift number on each letter used.

It is very easy to understand and use, but despite this, it took 300 years before anyone was able to successfully break it!

Many more complex ciphers (like Enigma) are based on the ever-changing Vigenère cipher which swaps one letter for another in a specific pattern.

To encode or decode it's helpful to have a Vigenère square handy.

	A	B	C	D	E	F	G	H	I	J	K	L	M	N	O	P	Q	R	S	T	U	V	W	X	Y	Z
A	A	B	C	D	E	F	G	H	I	J	K	L	M	N	O	P	Q	R	S	T	U	V	W	X	Y	Z
B	B	C	D	E	F	G	H	I	J	K	L	M	N	O	P	Q	R	S	T	U	V	W	X	Y	Z	A
C	C	D	E	F	G	H	I	J	K	L	M	N	O	P	Q	R	S	T	U	V	W	X	Y	Z	A	B
D	D	E	F	G	H	I	J	K	L	M	N	O	P	Q	R	S	T	U	V	W	X	Y	Z	A	B	C
E	E	F	G	H	I	J	K	L	M	N	O	P	Q	R	S	T	U	V	W	X	Y	Z	A	B	C	D
F	F	G	H	I	J	K	L	M	N	O	P	Q	R	S	T	U	V	W	X	Y	Z	A	B	C	D	E
G	G	H	I	J	K	L	M	N	O	P	Q	R	S	T	U	V	W	X	Y	Z	A	B	C	D	E	F
H	H	I	J	K	L	M	N	O	P	Q	R	S	T	U	V	W	X	Y	Z	A	B	C	D	E	F	G
I	I	J	K	L	M	N	O	P	Q	R	S	T	U	V	W	X	Y	Z	A	B	C	D	E	F	G	H
J	J	K	L	M	N	O	P	Q	R	S	T	U	V	W	X	Y	Z	A	B	C	D	E	F	G	H	I
K	K	L	M	N	O	P	Q	R	S	T	U	V	W	X	Y	Z	A	B	C	D	E	F	G	H	I	J
L	L	M	N	O	P	Q	R	S	T	U	V	W	X	Y	Z	A	B	C	D	E	F	G	H	I	J	K
M	M	N	O	P	Q	R	S	T	U	V	W	X	Y	Z	A	B	C	D	E	F	G	H	I	J	K	L
N	N	O	P	Q	R	S	T	U	V	W	X	Y	Z	A	B	C	D	E	F	G	H	I	J	K	L	M
O	O	P	Q	R	S	T	U	V	W	X	Y	Z	A	B	C	D	E	F	G	H	I	J	K	L	M	N
P	P	Q	R	S	T	U	V	W	X	Y	Z	A	B	C	D	E	F	G	H	I	J	K	L	M	N	O
Q	Q	R	S	T	U	V	W	X	Y	Z	A	B	C	D	E	F	G	H	I	J	K	L	M	N	O	P
R	R	S	T	U	V	W	X	Y	Z	A	B	C	D	E	F	G	H	I	J	K	L	M	N	O	P	Q
S	S	T	U	V	W	X	Y	Z	A	B	C	D	E	F	G	H	I	J	K	L	M	N	O	P	Q	R
T	T	U	V	W	X	Y	Z	A	B	C	D	E	F	G	H	I	J	K	L	M	N	O	P	Q	R	S
U	U	V	W	X	Y	Z	A	B	C	D	E	F	G	H	I	J	K	L	M	N	O	P	Q	R	S	T
V	V	W	X	Y	Z	A	B	C	D	E	F	G	H	I	J	K	L	M	N	O	P	Q	R	S	T	U
W	W	X	Y	Z	A	B	C	D	E	F	G	H	I	J	K	L	M	N	O	P	Q	R	S	T	U	V
X	X	Y	Z	A	B	C	D	E	F	G	H	I	J	K	L	M	N	O	P	Q	R	S	T	U	V	W
Y	Y	Z	B	B	C	D	E	F	G	H	I	J	K	L	M	N	O	P	Q	R	S	T	U	V	W	X
Z	Z	A	C	C	D	E	F	G	H	I	J	K	L	M	N	O	P	Q	R	S	T	U	V	W	X	Y

How do you crack a Vigenère Cipher?

It's probably easiest to explain how you encode the text first so that you can then understand how you would reverse it.

First, you need to decide on the code words/sentences you want to use. These need to be known by your receiver. So, if you are transmitting in Vigenère code, you also need to find a method of transmitting the code word.

For the explanation, we're using the code word, "Pigsmightfly". To make it easier to encode, I've highlighted the letters I'll be using on the Vigenère square.

	A	B	C	D	E	F	G	H	I	J	K	L	M	N	O	P	Q	R	S	T	U	V	W	X	Y	Z
A	A	B	C	D	E	F	G	H	I	J	K	L	M	N	O	P	Q	R	S	T	U	V	W	X	Y	Z
B	B	C	D	E	F	G	H	I	J	K	L	M	N	O	P	Q	R	S	T	U	V	W	X	Y	Z	A
C	C	D	E	F	G	H	I	J	K	L	M	N	O	P	Q	R	S	T	U	V	W	X	Y	Z	A	B
D	D	E	F	G	H	I	J	K	L	M	N	O	P	Q	R	S	T	U	V	W	X	Y	Z	A	B	C
E	E	F	G	H	I	J	K	L	M	N	O	P	Q	R	S	T	U	V	W	X	Y	Z	A	B	C	D
F	F	G	H	I	J	K	L	M	N	O	P	Q	R	S	T	U	V	W	X	Y	Z	A	B	C	D	E
G	G	H	I	J	K	L	M	N	O	P	Q	R	S	T	U	V	W	X	Y	Z	A	B	C	D	E	F
H	H	I	J	K	L	M	N	O	P	Q	R	S	T	U	V	W	X	Y	Z	A	B	C	D	E	F	G
I	I	J	K	L	M	N	O	P	Q	R	S	T	U	V	W	X	Y	Z	A	B	C	D	E	F	G	H
J	J	K	L	M	N	O	P	Q	R	S	T	U	V	W	X	Y	Z	A	B	C	D	E	F	G	H	I
K	K	L	M	N	O	P	Q	R	S	T	U	V	W	X	Y	Z	A	B	C	D	E	F	G	H	I	J
L	L	M	N	O	P	Q	R	S	T	U	V	W	X	Y	Z	A	B	C	D	E	F	G	H	I	J	K
M	M	N	O	P	Q	R	S	T	U	V	W	X	Y	Z	A	B	C	D	E	F	G	H	I	J	K	L
N	N	O	P	Q	R	S	T	U	V	W	X	Y	Z	A	B	C	D	E	F	G	H	I	J	K	L	M
O	O	P	Q	R	S	T	U	V	W	X	Y	Z	A	B	C	D	E	F	G	H	I	J	K	L	M	N
P	P	Q	R	S	T	U	V	W	X	Y	Z	A	B	C	D	E	F	G	H	I	J	K	L	M	N	O
Q	Q	R	S	T	U	V	W	X	Y	Z	A	B	C	D	E	F	G	H	I	J	K	L	M	N	O	P
R	R	S	T	U	V	W	X	Y	Z	A	B	C	D	E	F	G	H	I	J	K	L	M	N	O	P	Q
S	S	T	U	V	W	X	Y	Z	A	B	C	D	E	F	G	H	I	J	K	L	M	N	O	P	Q	R
T	T	U	V	W	X	Y	Z	A	B	C	D	E	F	G	H	I	J	K	L	M	N	O	P	Q	R	S
U	U	V	W	X	Y	Z	A	B	C	D	E	F	G	H	I	J	K	L	M	N	O	P	Q	R	S	T
V	V	W	X	Y	Z	A	B	C	D	E	F	G	H	I	J	K	L	M	N	O	P	Q	R	S	T	U
W	W	X	Y	Z	A	B	C	D	E	F	G	H	I	J	K	L	M	N	O	P	Q	R	S	T	U	V
X	X	Y	Z	A	B	C	D	E	F	G	H	I	J	K	L	M	N	O	P	Q	R	S	T	U	V	W
Y	Y	Z	B	B	C	D	F	F	G	H	I	J	K	L	M	N	O	P	Q	R	S	T	U	V	W	X
Z	Z	A	C	C	D	E	F	G	H	I	J	K	L	M	N	O	P	Q	R	S	T	U	V	W	X	Y

You then decide on the message you want to send. In this case, Jo loves Floss.

Write your ciphertext underneath the message so you know which letters provide the combination shift.

P I G S M I G H T F L Y
J O L O V E S F L O S S

If your code is shorter than the message you want to write, all you do is repeat the code word so that all letters are matched.

Taking the example above: to encode the letter J, you will be using the 'P' line. To encode the letter O, you will be using the 'I' line, and so on. Use the grid to cross-reference the two letters – the one from the code word with the one with the text you want to encode – to create a whole new coded letter. In this case, the J and P cross at the Y.

	A	B	C	D	E	F	G	H	I	J	K	L	M	N	O	P	Q	R	S	T	U	V	W	X	Y	Z
A	A	B	C	D	E	F	G	H	I	J	K	L	M	N	O	P	Q	R	S	T	U	V	W	X	Y	Z
B	B	C	D	E	F	G	H	I	J	K	L	M	N	O	P	Q	R	S	T	U	V	W	X	Y	Z	A
C	C	D	E	F	G	H	I	J	K	L	M	N	O	P	Q	R	S	T	U	V	W	X	Y	Z	A	B
D	D	E	F	G	H	I	J	K	L	M	N	O	P	Q	R	S	T	U	V	W	X	Y	Z	A	B	C
E	E	F	G	H	I	J	K	L	M	N	O	P	Q	R	S	T	U	V	W	X	Y	Z	A	B	C	D
F	F	G	H	I	J	K	L	M	N	O	P	Q	R	S	T	U	V	W	X	Y	Z	A	B	C	D	E
G	G	H	I	J	K	L	M	N	O	P	Q	R	S	T	U	V	W	X	Y	Z	A	B	C	D	E	F
H	H	I	J	K	L	M	N	O	P	Q	R	S	T	U	V	W	X	Y	Z	A	B	C	D	E	F	G
I	I	J	K	L	M	N	O	P	Q	R	S	T	U	V	W	X	Y	Z	A	B	C	D	E	F	G	H
J	J	K	L	M	N	O	P	Q	R	S	T	U	V	W	X	Y	Z	A	B	C	D	E	F	G	H	I
K	K	L	M	N	O	P	Q	R	S	T	U	V	W	X	Y	Z	A	B	C	D	E	F	G	H	I	J
L	L	M	N	O	P	Q	R	S	T	U	V	W	X	Y	Z	A	B	C	D	E	F	G	H	I	J	K
M	M	N	O	P	Q	R	S	T	U	V	W	X	Y	Z	A	B	C	D	E	F	G	H	I	J	K	L
N	N	O	P	Q	R	S	T	U	V	W	X	Y	Z	A	B	C	D	E	F	G	H	I	J	K	L	M
O	O	P	Q	R	S	T	U	V	W	X	Y	Z	A	B	C	D	E	F	G	H	I	J	K	L	M	N
P	P	Q	R	S	T	U	V	W	X	Y	Z	A	B	C	D	E	F	G	H	I	J	K	L	M	N	O
Q	Q	R	S	T	U	V	W	X	Y	Z	A	B	C	D	E	F	G	H	I	J	K	L	M	N	O	P

Sometimes it's easier if you have a "set square" cut out of paper which you can lay over the grid. That way you can easily cross reference without getting lost in the mass of letters.

Using the grid and the cross-references, this means your final message becomes:

P	I	G	S	M	I	G	H	T	F	L	Y	- Message
J	O	L	O	V	E	S	F	L	O	S	S	– Code word
Y	W	R	G	H	M	Y	M	E	T	D	Q	- Cipher text

If grid squares aren't your thing, you could recreate a moving Vigenère cipher with a simple code wheel, setting the code letters so that the letter 'A' matches the correct letter of your code word and then reading the new letter from the inner wheel.

To decrypt Vigenère, you work exactly in reverse. Write out the code word, write out the encrypted message and then cross-reference it using the internal square to read off the original message on the outer edge of the grid.

Try to decode the following two messages:

1) xhie mq bp's nlzmmsibp hpaok?
   Keyword = BAILEYS
2) zs nkx htdcgjychr ftoi jzujgywi
   Keyword = DONTTELLASOUL

Column Ciphers

Column, or poem ciphers, have been used by intelligence services for many years and like Vigenère ciphers they require shared knowledge of a code word.

How do you make column ciphers?

The first step in creating a column cipher is to decide on the word you plan to use. Intelligence agents will often use a long word from a book which has been agreed upon, or a long word from a memorized poem.

In the past, popular poems of the age were often used, but as they were published, it meant the enemy could easily decode the messages.

Eventually, the intelligence services created poetry of their own that they would memorize. Doing this meant the code word could never be learned as the source poem was never published!

As an example, we'll look at this limerick:

There was an old man from Nantucket,
Who kept all his cash in a bucket,
But his daughter named Nan,
Ran away with a man,
And as for the bucket, Nantucket.

From this limerick, we'll use the word "Nantucket" to encode our message "I want to be a super sleuth".

The first step in a column cipher is to create a grid that is as long as the code word. If Nantucket is our code word then our grid needs to be 9 letters long. One the grid is made, we then simply fill in the message writing left to right within the available boxes.

N	A	N	T	U	C	K	E	T
I	W	A	N	T	T	O	B	E
A	S	U	P	E	R	S	L	E
U	T	H	X	X	X	X	X	X

Any spare squares in the grid should be filled in using a hyphen, an unused letter (X in this case) or any other character – there should be no blanks.

Now we reorder the grid so that each column headed by our code word is placed in alphabetical order. So column A of Nantucket goes first, C second etc.

A	C	E	K	N	N	T	T	U
W	T	B	O	I	A	N	E	T
S	R	L	S	A	U	P	E	E
T	X	X	X	U	H	X	X	X

Traditionally, column ciphers would be read horizontally, so your message would say:

WTBOIANETSRLSAUPEETXXXUHXXX

However, you can also be sneaky and read vertically instead, making the message this:

WSTTRXBLXOSXIAUAUHNPXEEXTEX

As long as both the receiver and the encoder know which way the codes are being provided and read, they will get the right answer, but you may find you need to try both methods to see which works for your message.

Hint: If it's a vertical read, you need to know how long the message is to work out how many rows you will need.

Have a go at these:

Flying unsteadily and flapping their wings,
Butterflies **fluttering** are incredible things.
Whether Painted Lady or Clouded Yellow,
When you see one, say hello.

You need to decode the following:
ACAUOLGRTNOLSIONSNOOVIRIFGYUNPR-ESRCIHT

She **pondered** the question,
What could it mean?
A trick or a cipher,
Who'd be so mean?

You need to decode the following:

LCTIWAIEKVLSSRDRACLCPNCDLTEELUITOYCEODRNRR
WYEEYTAOANAEAH

Extra sneaky

It was very common for secret agents to double encode messages. After the column cipher was discovered, people realised that in its basic form it wasn't the most secure form of communication. Any column cipher could be read off column by column, meaning that if a person knew the correct dimensions needed to create the grid, it was very easy to decode by looking for anagram words.

Shuffling the order of letters began to provide extra security. And, as well as double encoding the cipher using another keyword, cryptographers also began to use column ciphers in conjunction with other ciphers.

The German military used double columnar transposition during both World Wars. This method was also used by resistance groups in occupied countries.

One-time Cipher Pads

One-time cipher pads are one of the most difficult ciphers to solve as they rely on both the sender and receiver having the same pre-shared key that is longer than any message likely to be sent. One-time cipher pads were originally described in 1882, then later reinvented in 1917 by Gilbert Vernam and Joseph Mauborgne. When used correctly, they are impossible to decrypt.

When one-time cipher pads are used, they are meant to be destroyed immediately so that enemies cannot intercept any messages. Usually, after a single message is sent, the key is changed. However in a lot of mystery subscription series, like CosyKiller, the box manufacturers make things *slightly* easier by keeping the same encryption key throughout. That means you just need to find out what it is that both the sender and receiver are using as their shared pad, and with time, you can decode all the communication.

To make one-time ciphers easier to work with, most agencies use blocks of letters or numbers so that fewer transcription errors occur. So, if you spot blocks of letters, chances are you're looking at a one-time cipher.

How do they work?

One-time ciphers work by converting letters into numbers and back again.

The key needs to be the same size or longer than the message that needs to be encrypted.

Both the message you want to write and the one time key need to be converted into numbers (A=1, B=2, etc.)

If your one-time cipher code was going to be a message like:

Onetimecipherssstink

Your numerical code would be:

15 14 5 20 9 13 5 3 9 16 8 5 18 19 19 20 9 14 11

You would then need to do the same for your actual message. If you wanted to send a message to a friend that read, "I hate ciphers", your numerical code would read:

9 8 1 20 5 3 9 16 8 5 18 19

It is important to write all of your numbers directly above each other so you can easily work with them, as one mistake throws out the entire code. In this example we don't need the full one time cipher code, so we've just used as much as we need:

15	14	5	20	9	13	5	3	9	16	8	5
9	8	1	20	5	3	9	16	8	5	18	19

Once your one time pad and message are lined up, the next step is to add the numbers together.

15+9 gives you your first NEW letter of the encrypted message.

15+9 = 24 – the letter X.

14+ 8 gives you your second encrypted number – 22 - which is V.

And so on.

If you end up with a sum that is greater than the number of characters in the alphabet e.g. 20+20, you subtract 26 from the number and your encrypted number becomes 14.

Once your line of ciphertext numbers is created, the next step is to turn those numbers back into letters again.

15	14	5	20	9	13	5	3	9	16	8	5
9	8	1	20	5	3	9	16	8	5	18	19
24	22	6	40	14	16	14	19	17	21	26	24
			14	This number is greater than 26, so we have taken 26 from the total to give us 14							
Y	W	G	O	O	Q	O	T	R	V	A	Y

To decrypt, you just do the same in reverse, but this time subtracting your cipher from the encrypted message. This will occasionally give you a minus number, but all you need to do is add on 26 to get back to the number it should be and convert it back into letters.

When it comes to a shared pad, if those sending and receiving messages aren't using a specific one time cipher pad generated by their agency, then it helps to find something that both people may own. Sometimes this might be a specific passage in a bible or a book.

Why not have a go at deciphering the code below.

The poem used in the cipher:

Roses are red,
Violets aren't blue.
I don't mind ciphers,
How about you?

Now try deciphering this:

ADYYX OFJWI LAUEI NNADG RWHIG KBRXW QIQNG WRVOK TOHZZ BSUWZ FOBZ

Rail Fence Ciphers

A rail fence cipher is an easy to apply cipher that jumbles up the order of the letters of a message in a quick, convenient way.

The security of a key is used to make the cipher more difficult to break. It works by writing your message on alternate lines across the page, and then reading off each line in turn.

Simple rail fence ciphers exist where each letter in the code is written in a zigzag pattern across the page, and the ciphertext is then read off by writing the top row first, followed by the bottom row.

In this example, the plaintext says, "Rail fence cipher", but the encryption reads "RIFNEIHRALECCPE", like this:

R		I		F		N		E		I		H		R
	A		L		E		C		C		P		E	

When encrypting any message, you need to have a key. For a rail fence cipher, it is the number of rows used. You can then start writing the letters of the plaintext diagonally down to the right until you reach the number of rows specified by the key. Then work your way back to the top and continue in this manner until the end of the message.

Decrypting rail fence ciphers involves reconstructing the diagonal grid used to encode the message. For this example, we'll decode the following:

DIAATOLKNCDSOYUEIOAONOPLR (4)

Start by making a grid with the same number of rows in it as the key indicates (in this case that would be 4), and as many columns as the length of the ciphertext (25).

To begin the grid, place the letter 'D' in the first available space and then diagonally place dashes (-) up and down until you have reached the top of the grid again. This is where you would then place the letter 'I'.

You would then repeat this process until you have completed each row and used each letter in your ciphertext. The process can be seen below:

D						I						A						A						T
	-				-		-				-		-				-		-				-	
		-		-				-		-				-		-				-		-		
			-						-						-						-			

The next letter will go on the second line, and one box along from the first letter, as below:

D						I						A						A						T
	O				L		K				N		C				D		S				O	
		-		-				-		-				-		-				-		-		
			-						-						-						-			

The next letter starts on the third row.

D						I						A						A						T
	O				L		K				N		C				D		S				O	
		Y		U				E		I				O		A				O		N		
			-						-						-						-			

The remaining letters go on the bottom line of squares.

D						I						A						A						T
	O				L		K				N		C				D		S				O	
		Y		U				E		I				O		A				O		N		
			O						P						L						R			

Now we can see that the plaintext reads: “Do you like pina coladas or not”.

Now see if you can encode the following message:

I knew you could do it (3)

ADFGVX Cipher

The ADFGVX cipher was used by the German Army during WWI and was an extension of an earlier cipher, the ADFGX cipher. It is a fractionating transposition cipher that combines a Polybius square (Knock code style cipher) with a columnar transposition. It is named ADFGVX after the six letters used in the ciphertext. These were chosen deliberately as they sound dissimilar when transmitted via morse code.

The key square is a 6x6 square containing all the letters in the alphabet and the numbers 0-9. They can be put anywhere in the square and in any order you like.

To encode a message using ADFGVX, you first need to build a table like the one below:

	A	D	F	G	V	X
A	U	E	H	N	7	1
D	T	2	P	C	A	3
F	W	X	9	R	Q	F
G	O	8	4	D	I	Z
V	B	G	K	6	5	V
X	J	L	M	S	Y	0

To code the message you use the XY axis to give you a two-letter code. For example, the message 'I will escape' would become:

I	W	I	L	L	E	S	C	A	P	E
GV	FA	GV	XD	XD	AD	XG	DG	DV	DF	AD

The ciphertext is now twice as long as the plaintext, but could still be solved quite easily using simple letter substitution.

At this point the message is encoded again.

Using a keyword to create the columns, the coded message is now written with the letters pairs broken up underneath. This is known as fractionating. Using the code word 'ENIGMA', the letters are written across the columns, not down, like this:

E	N	I	G	M	A
G	V	F	A	G	V
X	D	X	D	A	D
X	G	D	G	D	V
D	F	A	D	-	-

As the message doesn't fit exactly, hyphens or unused letters are added to fill the columns. Using the code word as a guide, the columns are then rearranged into alphabetical order. This gives us:

A	E	G	I	M	N
V	G	A	F	G	V
D	X	D	X	A	D
V	X	G	D	D	G
-	D	D	A	-	F

The final ciphertext is then read off in columns, meaning our original message has now become:

'VDV-GXXDADGDFXDAGAD-VDGF'

This type of cipher can present many problems to those trying to decipher them. Unlike column ciphers, they cannot easily be broken by anagramming to see which words appear. The initial substitution step using the matrix to provide two letters for each letter makes it almost impossible to break without the code word.

Using the alphabet shown earlier, have a go at encrypting the following message:

1) DIFFICULT CODE
Keyword is DANGER

Porta Cipher

Giovanni Battista Della Porta was an Italian scholar who, during the Spanish Inquisition, found ways to communicate with his friends who had been imprisoned. One of the methods Della Porta adopted was to write secret messages on the inside of eggs. Using a mixture of alum and plant pigments, he would write messages on eggshells and then boil the eggs. As eggshells are semi-porous, the ink penetrated the shell, but when boiled in water, the ink on the outside of the egg disappeared leaving the message now only visible on the egg white!

Della Porta was also responsible for inventing what is known as the Porta Cipher. The Porta cipher is a bit like the Vigenère cipher, but it uses only a 13-letter alphabet, doubling each letter on the X axis. The cipher square is set out in the following way:

Keys	A	B	C	D	E	F	G	H	I	J	K	L	M	N	O	P	Q	R	S	T	U	V	W	X	Y	Z
AB	n	o	p	q	r	s	t	u	v	w	x	y	z	a	b	c	d	e	f	g	h	I	j	k	l	m
CD	o	p	q	r	s	t	u	v	w	x	y	z	n	m	a	b	c	d	e	f	g	H	i	j	k	l
EF	p	q	r	s	t	u	v	w	x	y	z	n	o	l	m	a	b	c	d	e	f	G	h	i	j	k
GH	q	r	s	t	u	v	w	x	y	z	n	o	p	k	l	m	a	b	c	d	e	F	g	h	i	j
IJ	r	s	t	u	v	w	x	y	z	n	o	p	q	j	k	l	m	a	b	c	d	E	f	g	h	i
KL	s	t	u	v	w	x	y	z	n	o	p	q	r	i	j	k	l	m	a	b	c	D	e	f	g	h
MN	t	u	v	w	x	y	z	n	o	p	q	r	s	h	i	j	k	l	m	a	b	C	d	e	f	g
OP	u	v	w	x	y	z	n	o	p	q	r	s	t	g	h	i	j	k	l	m	a	B	c	d	e	f
QR	v	w	x	y	z	n	o	p	q	r	s	t	u	f	g	h	i	j	k	l	m	A	b	c	d	e
ST	w	x	y	z	n	o	p	q	r	s	t	u	v	e	f	g	h	i	j	k	l	M	a	b	c	d
UV	x	y	z	n	o	p	q	r	s	t	u	v	w	d	e	f	g	h	i	j	k	L	m	a	b	c
WX	y	z	n	o	p	q	r	s	t	u	v	w	x	c	d	e	f	g	h	i	j	K	l	m	a	b
YZ	z	n	o	p	q	r	s	t	u	v	w	x	y	b	c	d	e	f	g	h	i	J	k	l	m	a

Porta ciphers use a keyword. For this example, we will use the word "Decrypt", repeating the keyword above our plaintext to encipher it, like this:

D E C R Y P T D E C R Y P T D E C R Y

A N O T H E R C I P H E R S O L V E D

We take the first letter, 'D', and find it on the first column

(CD), then move along this row of the table until we come to the column with the 'A' at the top. This intersection gives our ciphertext the character 'O'. The next letter is 'E', the first column is 'EF' and we follow it along to the 'N' on the top row, making our intersection letter 'L'.
The plaintext therefore becomes:

'OLALTYIQXBPQKJANHZP'

See if you can encrypt the following plaintexts:

1) HOW DO YOU FIND OUT YOU CAN WRITE ON THE INSIDE OF EGGS

Keyword is BIZARRE

2) I'M OFF TO FIND SOME ALUM

Keyword is EUREKA

Straddling Checkerboard Cipher

The straddling checkerboard cipher uses numbers to replace letters. To begin with, a table is set up with the Y axis going from 0-9 and the X axis consisting of three rows, the first of which is blank and the second and third are two random single digit numbers(in this case 3 and 7). The alphabet is then entered into the grid using a random permutation as its key. In this instance, we have used the following order:

'XQJAEINUPBOFHTYVMKSLWGRCDZ'

However, the first row has the numbers 3 and 7 left blank. Using this information, a straddling checkerboard is set up and looks like this:

	0	1	2	3	4	5	6	7	8	9
	X	Q	J		A	E	I		N	U
3	P	B	O	F	H	T	Y	V	M	K
7	S	L	W	G	R	C	D	Z		

As you can see, the top row is set up with the first eight key letters (XQJAEINU), leaving two blank spots in the 3 and 7 columns. Don't forget, the column numbers don't have to be 3 and 7 - they could be any number the encoder chooses.

The second and third rows are labelled with the two digits from the blank spaces in the top row (3 and 7), then filled with the remaining key letters.

No doubt you've noticed there are two spare letters in the two numbered rows. In this example, they are at the end of the last row, but they can go anywhere as long as both sender and receiver use the same system.

To encipher, a letter on the top row is replaced by the number labelling its column, so 'Q' would become '1'. Letters on the other rows are replaced by both their row number and column number, so 'W' would become '72', 'M' would become '38' and so on.

Let's encode the phrase "You are a super sleuth":

Y	O	U	A	R	E	A	S	U	P	E	R	S	L	E	U	T	H
3 6	3 2	9	4	7 4	5	4	7 0	9	3 0	5	7 4	7 0	7 1	5	9	3 5	3 4

Taking the numbers from the table above, the phrase 'you are super sleuth' becomes:

36329474547093057470715935 34

The cipher may be sent like this, but quite often straddling checkerboard ciphers are double encoded. This may be through a substitution or transposition step.

See how you get on with these:

1) Set up a straddling checkerboard using the following order:

   BNQAWDSKZCLVUMETIJRGOXPFYH

	0	1	2	3	4	5	6	7	8	9
1										
6										

Now encode the following messages using the above key:

2) MY BRAIN IS TURNING TO JELLY
3) I THINK I NEED A BREAK

Polygraphic Substitution Ciphers

Félix-Marie Delastelle, a French cryptographer, loved creating ciphers as a hobby. Unlike most people who worked in the field of cryptography (academics, military, diplomats), Delastelle worked at a port. His main contributions to the creation of ciphers included fractionation and transposition. He also created the Bifid cipher, the Trifid cipher and the Four-Square cipher.

Bifid Cipher

Bifids are often used by amateur cryptographers and their keys consist of a 25 letter 'key square'. The alphabet is entered randomly into the grid, and 'I' and 'J' are merged in the key square as below:

	1	2	3	4	5
1	T	H	E	Q	U
2	I/J	C	K	B	R
3	O	W	N	F	X
4	M	P	S	V	L
5	A	Z	Y	D	G

When enciphering plaintext, each letter is replaced by the numbers on the left-hand side and top of the key square.

These are then written on top of one another, so a 'D' would be written in this way:

5

4

For this example, we shall encode the plaintext, 'Curiosity killed the cat':

	C	U	R	I	O	S	I	T	Y	K	I	L	L	E	D	T	H	E	C	A	T
ROW	2	1	2	2	3	4	2	1	5	2	2	4	4	1	5	1	1	1	2	5	1
COL	2	5	5	1	1	3	1	1	3	3	1	5	5	3	4	1	2	3	2	1	1

The groups are then read off from left to right. This is the fractionating step as it separates the row number and column number. It gives us the following sequence of numbers:

21 22 34 21 52 24 41 51 11 25 12 55 11 31 13 31 55 34 13 32 11

This new sequence is then re-enciphered using the original alphabet key-square to give us the following cipher:

I C F I Z B M A T R H G T O E O G F E W T

Longer messages are traditionally broken up into what is called a "period", and the fractioning is applied to each "period" individually. Periods are traditionally 5-20 numbers in length. If we were to apply a period to this code of 5, then the number sequence would be very different:

	C	U	R	I	O	S	I	T	Y	K	I	L	L	E	D	T	H	E	C	A	T
ROW	2	1	2	2	3	4	2	1	5	2	2	4	4	1	5	1	1	1	2	5	1
COL	2	5	5	1	1	3	1	1	3	3	1	5	5	3	4	1	2	3	2	1	1

This period of 5 would make the numbers:

21 22 32 55 11 42 15 23 11 33 41 51 55 34 11 12 51 23 21 11

Which would make the enciphered text:

I C W G T P U C T N M A G F T H A K I T

Using the key square shown earlier, why not have a go at coding this message:

THETIMEHASCOMETOLEAVE

1)

	T	H	E	I	I	M	F	H	A	S	C	O	M	E	T	O	L	E	A	V	E
ROW																					
COL																					

2) Now create the number sequence using a period of 6.
3) Now re-encipher the numbers into letters for the final code.

Trifid Cipher

The Trifid cipher is similar to the Bifid cipher and combines substitution with transposition and fractionation. However unlike the Bifid cipher, which uses a 5x5 key-square, the Trifid cipher uses three 3x3x3 key squares.

The key is once again a random permutation of the alphabet, placed in the form of three squares. The full stop makes up the 27th space in our squares.

For this example, the alphabet we will use is:

KUZHSXPVR.ILBOEYFAWQDGCNJMT

Filling the three squares horizontally and one at a time, they would therefore look like this:

	1	2	3
1	K	U	Z
2	H	S	X
3	P	V	R

	1	2	3
1	.	I	L
2	B	O	E
3	Y	F	A

	1	2	3
1	W	D	Q
2	G	C	N
3	J	M	T

As an example, we will encipher the text, 'Learning all these ciphers is hard'.

The first step requires locating the plaintext letters in the squares. L is in square 2, row 1, column 3, so becomes 213. If we do the same thing with the letter E, it becomes 223.

We now write down the numbers corresponding to each letter vertically so we can see it more clearly:

L	E	A	R	N	I	N	G	A	L	L	T	H	E	S	E	C	I	P	H	E	R	S	I	S	H	A	R	D
2	2	2	1	3	2	3	3	2	2	2	3	1	2	1	2	3	2	1	1	2	1	1	2	1	1	2	1	3
1	2	3	3	2	1	2	2	3	1	1	3	2	2	2	2	2	1	3	2	2	3	2	1	2	2	3	3	1
3	3	3	3	3	2	3	1	3	3	3	3	1	3	2	3	2	2	1	1	3	3	2	2	2	1	3	3	2

At the moment, our cipher would still be fairly easy to break using letter substitution. So we are going to break it into periods of 6 and fraction each individual period:

L	E	A	R	N	I		N	G	A	L	L	T		H	E	S	E	C	I		P	H	E	R	S	I		S	H	A	R	D
2	2	2	1	3	2		3	3	2	2	2	3		1	2	1	2	3	2		1	1	2	1	1	2		1	1	2	1	3
1	2	3	3	2	1		2	2	3	1	1	3		2	2	2	2	2	1		3	2	2	3	2	1		2	2	3	3	1
3	3	3	3	3	2		3	1	3	3	3	3		1	3	2	3	2	2		1	1	3	3	2	2		2	1	3	3	2

This means our number sequence becomes:

222, 132, 123, 321, 333, 332, 332, 223, 223, 112, 313, 333, 121, 232, 222, 221, 132, 322, 112, 112, 322, 321, 113, 322, 112, 132, 233, 121, 332

With our new numbers we now use the Trifid squares to convert each sequence back to letters:

This gives us the cipher:

OVXGTMMEEZQTHFOBVCUUCGZCUVAHM

Using the 3x3x3 square shown earlier, try and encode the following message:

1) WHY ARE YOU LOOKING AT ME LIKE THAT

2) Now do the number sequence using a period of 7 and list the numbers.

3) Now re-encipher the numbers into letters for the final code.

Four-Square Cipher

As with the ADFGVX cipher, the four-square cipher encrypts pairs of letters. This makes it significantly more difficult than substitution ciphers and the use of four squares makes it much harder to break than the ADFGVX cipher.

This four-square cipher uses four 5x5 matrices arranged in a square. Each of the matrices contain 25 letters (as is usually the case, the letters I and J are merged, although some people have the letters C and K sharing a square). In most cases, the upper-left and lower-right matrices are the plaintext squares. These squares contain a standard alphabet. The upper-right and lower-left squares are the ciphertext squares. These squares contain an alphabet that has been arranged randomly and both squares have the alphabet arranged differently.

This four-square algorithm allows for two separate keys, one for each of the two ciphertext matrices.

Let's have a go at enciphering the following text:

'Bicycles have two wheels'.

The first thing to do is break up the plaintext into bigrams (letter pairs), so BICYCLES HAVE TWO WHEELS becomes BI CY CL ES HA VE TW OW HE EL SX.

Hopefully, you will have spotted that an 'X' has now been added at the end of the plaintext. This is to ensure that the ciphertext is of an even length.

Here are the four squares we will be using:

a	b	c	d	e
f	g	h	i/j	k
l	m	n	o	p
q	r	s	t	u
v	w	x	y	z

F	L	P	M	I/J
S	U	A	R	V
K	D	C	O	T
X	G	Q	E	Z
H	B	Y	N	W

C	K	S	B	X
R	N	U	W	V
I/J	H	D	F	Z
G	A	E	Y	M
O	P	T	L	Q

a	b	c	d	e
f	g	h	i/j	k
l	m	n	o	p
q	r	s	t	u
v	w	x	y	z

Using the four squares, locate the bigram (letter pair) to encrypt in the plain alphabet squares. For the bigram 'BI', the first letter is located in the top left square and the second letter is located in the bottom right square.

Draw a rectangle incorporating these letters using all four of the squares. In this case, the rectangle would start at the top left 'b', go across to the top right 'M', down to the bottom right 'i/j' and across to the bottom left 'N'. Using the letters in the opposite corners to the plaintext letters, this would make our 'BI' bigram become 'MN'. Similarly, for 'CY', our rectangle would be formed by 'c', 'M', 'y' and 'T', making our new bigram 'MT'.

a	b	c	d	e	F	L	P	M	I/J
f	g	h	i/j	k	S	U	A	R	V
l	m	n	o	p	K	D	C	O	T
q	r	s	t	u	X	G	Q	E	Z
v	w	x	y	z	H	B	Y	N	W
C	K	S	B	X	a	b	c	d	e
R	N	U	W	V	f	g	h	i/j	k
I/J	H	D	F	Z	l	m	n	o	p
G	A	E	Y	M	q	r	s	t	u
O	P	T	L	Q	v	w	x	y	z

If we repeat the process for the entire plaintext, 'Bicycles have two wheelsx' becomes the following:

MNMTFDPMSSWCGLDLVSFZQT

Using the squares above, try encoding this plaintext:

1) WHAT TIME CAN I EXPECT MY TRANSPORT

Other Ways to Hide Information

For years there have been many other ways to conceal information aside from written/typed codes.

Dead Drops

Dead drops have been used for many years. A package is dropped at a certain location, supposedly only known to both the agent and the individual supplying the information. Dead drops can take many forms, such as fake rocks, fake bricks, even dead rats...

Over time, as surveillance technology has improved, dead drops have also needed to incorporate the use of technology. Robert Hanssen, a disgraced FBI agent, mixed traditional methods with the knowledge working with the FBI gave him, and he mailed a disk to the KGB containing secret information he had gained. The disk had been reformatted by Hanssen using 40-track-mode. This gave the disk slightly less capacity than usual so that secret messages could be concealed in its lost space. He also used a Palm III handheld computer to communicate with the SVR (the KGB's successor agency) and used the same dead drop over twenty times! Hanssen ultimately received a life sentence without the possibility of parole after giving the KBG/SVR over 6,000 pages of valuable documentary material.

Signals

On many occasions, the use of dead drops was signalled by the agents involved using chalk marks on walls, moved objects, specific body language, even changes to habits (e.g. curtains pulled down in certain windows, lights switched on in specific places). Many of us remember Fox Mulder from the X Files placing his lamp in a specific way highlighting a cross on the window to request a meeting. Signals have always formed part of code transmission, alerting agents to the presence of coded messages or a desire to meet.

Code Phrases

Code phrases are another way to encrypt information. These can be used in conjunction with ciphers or simply used over regular communication channels if the phrase hasn't already been decoded.

Code phrases are so often used, we probably don't even realise they are ways of transmitting hidden messages. "Ask for Angela" is one very public campaign which means those at the bar know to get a female away from a difficult date if she asks to speak to Angela. But there are other phrases that are so well known now, they aren't very effective as secret methods of communication.

Ten codes are officially known as ten signals and are used in CB transmissions or law enforcement. "10-4" means "Message received" – which most people will have heard on popular TV shows.

"Code Blue" in some hospitals means there is a cardiac event, requiring a crash cart team.

"Code Adam" is regularly used in stores to alert staff there is a missing child.

Security services often use codewords for the people they protect. Before her death in 2022 Queen Elizabeth II was known as "London Bridge". On the event of her death the phrase "London Bridge is down" was used alert all those who needed to know she had died without mentioning it specifically.

In the military there are various code names or code phrases associated with operations. One you may have heard of is "Bandit" – which means identified enemy aircraft.

Using code phrases in conjunction which ciphers means

even if the message is decoded successfully, the actual message being sent may still not be understood.

During the war many operations were known by code names, and for spies trying to send messages home, there were whole strings of phrases in use to provide information that couldn't easily be understood.

Conclusion

This short handbook has taken you on a whistlestop tour of the fascinating world of ciphers. From the ancient Greeks to the modern-day; ciphers have shaped the course of history and played a pivotal role in the realms of diplomacy, espionage, and personal communication.

Hopefully you are now equipped with the tools and knowledge you need to crack codes and the final pages of this book contain some of the most commonly used letter substitution ciphers to give you a quick reference guide for future puzzle solving work.

With practice and perseverance, you will learn to recognize the telltale signs of substitution ciphers, transposition ciphers, and the more complex systems employed.

Ultimately, the study of ciphers is a testament to the enduring human desire for secrecy. In a world where information is increasingly digital and easily accessible, the art of encryption continues to evolve, adapting to the ever-present threat of prying eyes. As you close the final pages of this book, remember that the secrets of cryptography are not confined to the past; they are alive and well in the present and will undoubtedly shape the future.

We hope on finishing this book you will take up our invitation to embark on a lifelong journey of codebreaking and to experience for yourself the thrill of unlocking a hidden message, whether it be in a treasure hunt or a puzzle by mail.

If you've enjoyed learning about codes and ciphers, why not take the journey a step further and embark on Cosykiller, a mystery story delivered by mail which includes some of the codes explained in this book.

www.cosykiller.com

Useful Alphabets used in codes

Letter to Number Cipher

A = 1
B = 2
C = 3
D = 4
E = 5
F = 6
G = 7
H = 8
I = 9

J = 10
K = 11
L = 12
M = 13
N = 14
O = 15
P = 16
Q = 17
R = 18

S = 19
T = 20
U = 21
V = 22
W = 23
X = 24
Y = 25
Z = 26

Phonetic Alphabet

A = Alpha
B = Bravo
C = Charlie
D = Delta
E = Echo
F = Foxtrot
G = Golf
H = Hotel
I = India

J = Juliet
K = Kilo
L = Lima
M = Mike
N = November
O = Oscar
P = Papa
Q = Quebec
R = Romeo

S = Sierra
T = Tango
U = Uniform
V = Victor
W = Whisky
X = Xray
Y = Yankee
Z = Zulu

Atbash Cipher

A	B	C	D	E	F	G	H	I	J	K	L	M
↕	↕	↕	↕	↕	↕	↕	↕	↕	↕	↕	↕	↕
Z	Y	X	W	V	U	T	S	R	Q	P	O	N

Morse

A	• —	S	• • •
B	— • • •	T	—
C	— • — •	U	• • —
D	— • •	V	• • • —
E	•	W	• — —
F	• • — •	X	— • • —
G	— — •	Y	— • — —
H	• • • •	Z	— — • •
I	• •	1	• — — — —
J	• — — —	2	• • — — —
K	— • —	3	• • • — —
L	• — • •	4	• • • • —
M	— —	5	• • • • •
N	— •	6	— • • • •
O	— — —	7	— — • • •
P	• — — •	8	— — — • •
Q	— — • —	9	— — — — •
R	• — •	0	— — — — —

Braille

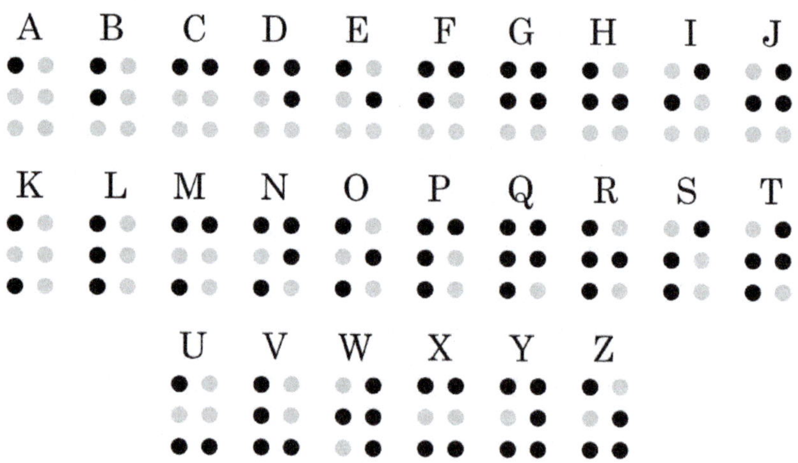

Semaphore

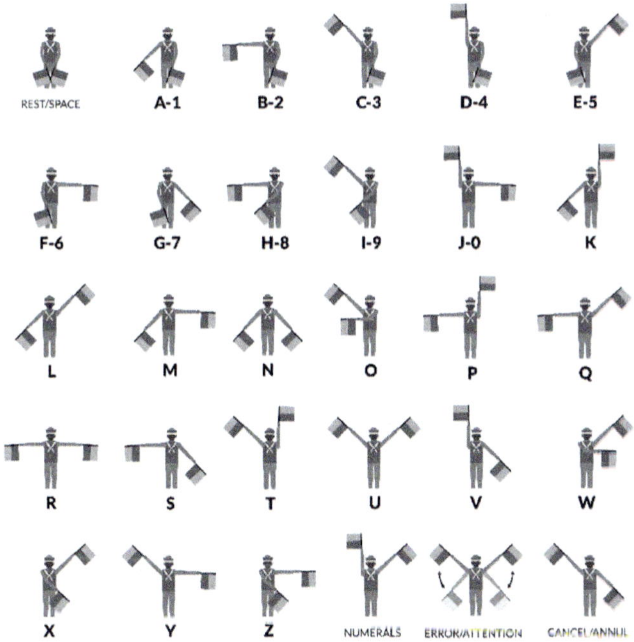

Dancing Men

Pig Pen

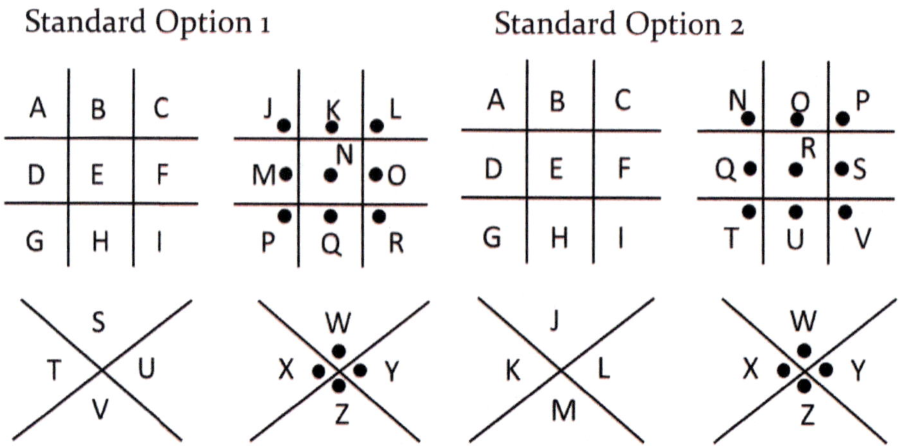

Templar

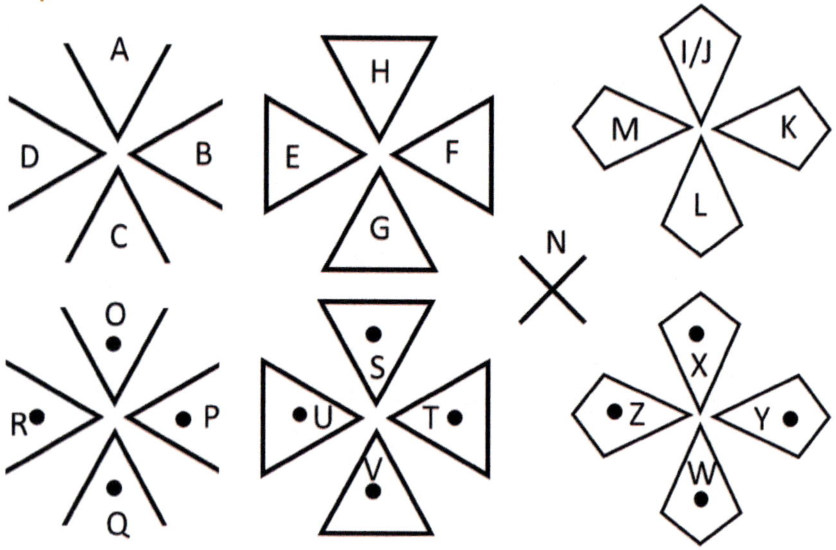

Nautical Flags

Moon

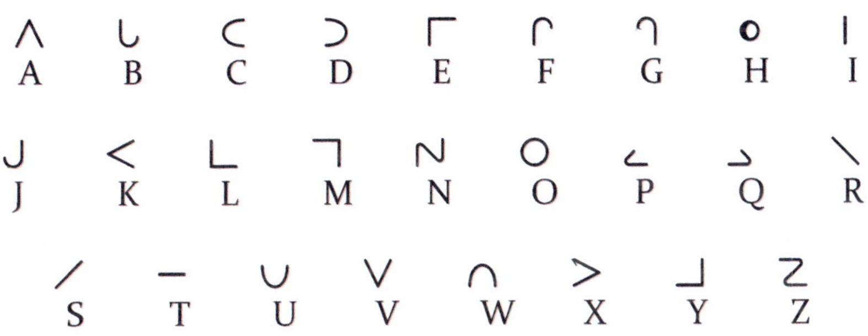

Hieroglyphics

letter substitution for English words

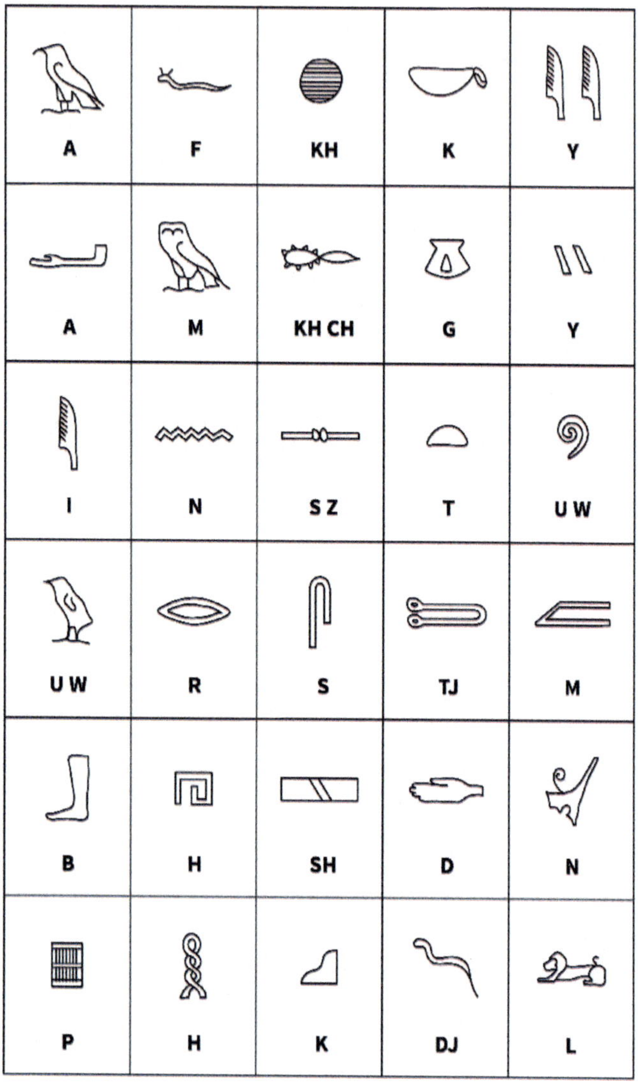

Runes

letter substitution for English words

Answers

Helpful Alphabets

Semaphore

1) THIS IS QUITE EASY

Morse Code

1) I RATHER LIKE DOING MORSE CODE
2) THERE ARE 12 MONTHS IN A YEAR

Pigpen Cipher

1) HOPE I GOT THIS CODE RIGHT

Templar Cipher

1) I BET THESE CODES GET HARDER

Dancing Men Cipher

1) THIS IS A BIT LIKE SEMAPHORE

Atbash Cipher

1) THIS CODE IS EASY TO BREAK

Caesar Cipher

1) Back 4 gives you I AM GETTING THE HANG OF THIS
2) First, turn the Morse Code into letters, then go back 3. Answer is MORSE CODE IS NOT THAT HARD REALLY
3) First, translate Pigpen into letters, then go back 1. Answer is PIGPEN IS EASY

Bacon cipher

1) THESE CIPHERS ARE MAKING ME HUNGRY

Secret words and messages

2) A letter home to a friend: The capital letters of each

sentence starting at the edge of the page read ACROSTIC.
3) Sightseeing in Cambridge: The letters in bold read GARDENS ARE DECENT.

Breaking Letter Substitution Codes

1) THE VIGINERE CIPHER WAS INVENTED IN FIFTEEN FIFTY THREE AND USED TO BE KNOWN AS THE UNBREAKABLE CIPHER
2) I HAVE ALWAYS WANTED TO GO TO PERU AND SEE MACHU PICCHU. THERE ARE OVER ONE HUNDRED FLIGHTS OF STAIRS. I BET IT'S EXHAUSTING.
3) IT GETS A LITTLE TRICKIER WHEN TWO LETTERS ARE USED TO REPRESENT ONE STOP WE HOPE THIS KNOCK CODE HAS NOT BEEN TOO DIFFICULT

Knock Codes

1) GI/AU/MT MI/NI/AR AU/MF/GU MR/AI/GI/GI/MT/NU GI/AU/MT NI/NF/MI OR/NI/NR/MF/NU
2) The Morse code translates to DO NOT ASK ME WHY, making the code MI/NI/ NU/NI/GI/ MF/GU/AT NR/MT OR/AU/OI

Playfair Code

1) The bigrams will become IW IL LN EX ED TO KE EP MY WI TS AB OU TM EX, making the answer UY LQ AK DY FE OP MD CS SI YU OT QD PQ SN DY

Vigenère Ciphers

1) WHAT IS JO'S FAVOURITE DRINK
2) WE ARE DISCOVERED SAVE YOURSELF

Column Ciphers

1) CONGRATULATIONS ON SOLVING YOUR FIRST CIPHER

2) WELL DONE YOU CRACKED IT AND VERTICALLY NOW LETS TRY A CAESAR CIPHER

Directional Codes

THESE PUZZLES SEEM TO GET RATHER TEDIOUS AFTER A WHILE BUT SOME ARE STILL OKAY

One-time Cipher Pads

1) I OFTEN NEED HELP WITH COMING UP WITH CODES SO MY COWORKERS HELP ME

Rail Fence Ciphers

1) IWCDTKEYUOLDINOUO

ADFGVX Ciphers

1) EXAGDAFADAFDDA-VVDA-GGXG-XGAE

Porta Cipher

1) UKK QG DMH WUAY GFG HCH XVL JAUGZ GL GYR VFKXQV CS ZOVF
2) X'W GUX GM PQLV FMWZ PQHO

Straddling Checkerboard Cipher

1)

	0	1	2	3	4	5	6	7	8	9
	B		N	Q	A	W		D	S	K
1	Z	C	L	V	U	M	E	T	I	J
6	R	G	O	X	P	F	Y	H		

2) 15660604182188171460218261176219161212066
3) 18176718291821616740601649

Bifid Cipher

1) Correct grid is:

	T	H	E	T	I	M	E	H	A	S	C	O	M	E	T	O	L	E	A	V	E
ROW	1	1	1	1	2	4	1	1	5	4	2	3	4	1	1	3	4	1	5	4	1
COL	1	2	3	1	1	1	3	2	1	3	2	1	1	3	1	1	5	2	1	4	2

2) 11 11 24 12 31 11 11 54 23 32 13 21 41 13 41 13 11 52 54 11 42

3) TTBHOTTDKWEIMEMETYDTS

Trifid Cipher

1) Correct grid is:

W	H	Y	A	R	E	Y	O	U	L	O	O	K	I	N	G	A	T	M	E	L	I	K	E	T	H	A	T
3	1	2	2	1	2	2	2	1	2	2	2	1	2	3	3	2	3	3	2	2	2	1	2	3	1	2	3
1	2	3	3	3	2	3	2	1	1	2	2	1	1	2	2	3	3	3	2	1	1	1	2	3	2	3	3
1	1	1	3	3	3	1	2	2	3	2	2	1	2	3	1	3	3	2	3	3	2	1	3	3	1	3	3

2) 312, 212, 212, 333, 231, 113, 331, 212, 221, 221, 122, 112, 232, 212, 332, 332, 222, 333, 213, 133, 233, 212, 312, 311, 232, 332, 133, 133

3) DIITYZJIBBSUFIMMOTLRAIWFMRR

Four-Square Cipher

1) YNMGEWTKFSOUPQTXMEOPGYPIZDDYQL

Vigenère Cipher Grid for practise work

	A	B	C	D	E	F	G	H	I	J	K	L	M	N	O	P	Q	R	S	T	U	V	W	X	Y	Z
A	A	B	C	D	E	F	G	H	I	J	K	L	M	N	O	P	Q	R	S	T	U	V	W	X	Y	Z
B	B	C	D	E	F	G	H	I	J	K	L	M	N	O	P	Q	R	S	T	U	V	W	X	Y	Z	A
C	C	D	E	F	G	H	I	J	K	L	M	N	O	P	Q	R	S	T	U	V	W	X	Y	Z	A	B
D	D	E	F	G	H	I	J	K	L	M	N	O	P	Q	R	S	T	U	V	W	X	Y	Z	A	B	C
E	E	F	G	H	I	J	K	L	M	N	O	P	Q	R	S	T	U	V	W	X	Y	Z	A	B	C	D
F	F	G	H	I	J	K	L	M	N	O	P	Q	R	S	T	U	V	W	X	Y	Z	A	B	C	D	E
G	G	H	I	J	K	L	M	N	O	P	Q	R	S	T	U	V	W	X	Y	Z	A	B	C	D	E	F
H	H	I	J	K	L	M	N	O	P	Q	R	S	T	U	V	W	X	Y	Z	A	B	C	D	E	F	G
I	I	J	K	L	M	N	O	P	Q	R	S	T	U	V	W	X	Y	Z	A	B	C	D	E	F	G	H
J	J	K	L	M	N	O	P	Q	R	S	T	U	V	W	X	Y	Z	A	B	C	D	E	F	G	H	I
K	K	L	M	N	O	P	Q	R	S	T	U	V	W	X	Y	Z	A	B	C	D	E	F	G	H	I	J
L	L	M	N	O	P	Q	R	S	T	U	V	W	X	Y	Z	A	B	C	D	E	F	G	H	I	J	K
M	M	N	O	P	Q	R	S	T	U	V	W	X	Y	Z	A	B	C	D	E	F	G	H	I	J	K	L
N	N	O	P	Q	R	S	T	U	V	W	X	Y	Z	A	B	C	D	E	F	G	H	I	J	K	L	M
O	O	P	Q	R	S	T	U	V	W	X	Y	Z	A	B	C	D	E	F	G	H	I	J	K	L	M	N
P	P	Q	R	S	T	U	V	W	X	Y	Z	A	B	C	D	E	F	G	H	I	J	K	L	M	N	O
Q	Q	R	S	T	U	V	W	X	Y	Z	A	B	C	D	E	F	G	H	I	J	K	L	M	N	O	P
R	R	S	T	U	V	W	X	Y	Z	A	B	C	D	E	F	G	H	I	J	K	L	M	N	O	P	Q
S	S	T	U	V	W	X	Y	Z	A	B	C	D	E	F	G	H	I	J	K	L	M	N	O	P	Q	R
T	T	U	V	W	X	Y	Z	A	B	C	D	E	F	G	H	I	J	K	L	M	N	O	P	Q	R	S
U	U	V	W	X	Y	Z	A	B	C	D	E	F	G	H	I	J	K	L	M	N	O	P	Q	R	S	T
V	V	W	X	Y	Z	A	B	C	D	E	F	G	H	I	J	K	L	M	N	O	P	Q	R	S	T	U
W	W	X	Y	Z	A	B	C	D	E	F	G	H	I	J	K	L	M	N	O	P	Q	R	S	T	U	V
X	X	Y	Z	A	B	C	D	E	F	G	H	I	J	K	L	M	N	O	P	Q	R	S	T	U	V	W
Y	Y	Z	B	B	C	D	E	F	G	H	I	J	K	L	M	N	O	P	Q	R	S	T	U	V	W	X
Z	Z	A	C	C	D	E	F	G	H	I	J	K	L	M	N	O	P	Q	R	S	T	U	V	W	X	Y

Vigenère Cipher Grid for practise work

	A	B	C	D	E	F	G	H	I	J	K	L	M	N	O	P	Q	R	S	T	U	V	W	X	Y	Z
A	A	B	C	D	E	F	G	H	I	J	K	L	M	N	O	P	Q	R	S	T	U	V	W	X	Y	Z
B	B	C	D	E	F	G	H	I	J	K	L	M	N	O	P	Q	R	S	T	U	V	W	X	Y	Z	A
C	C	D	E	F	G	H	I	J	K	L	M	N	O	P	Q	R	S	T	U	V	W	X	Y	Z	A	B
D	D	E	F	G	H	I	J	K	L	M	N	O	P	Q	R	S	T	U	V	W	X	Y	Z	A	B	C
E	E	F	G	H	I	J	K	L	M	N	O	P	Q	R	S	T	U	V	W	X	Y	Z	A	B	C	D
F	F	G	H	I	J	K	L	M	N	O	P	Q	R	S	T	U	V	W	X	Y	Z	A	B	C	D	E
G	G	H	I	J	K	L	M	N	O	P	Q	R	S	T	U	V	W	X	Y	Z	A	B	C	D	E	F
H	H	I	J	K	L	M	N	O	P	Q	R	S	T	U	V	W	X	Y	Z	A	B	C	D	E	F	G
I	I	J	K	L	M	N	O	P	Q	R	S	T	U	V	W	X	Y	Z	A	B	C	D	E	F	G	H
J	J	K	L	M	N	O	P	Q	R	S	T	U	V	W	X	Y	Z	A	B	C	D	E	F	G	H	I
K	K	L	M	N	O	P	Q	R	S	T	U	V	W	X	Y	Z	A	B	C	D	E	F	G	H	I	J
L	L	M	N	O	P	Q	R	S	T	U	V	W	X	Y	Z	A	B	C	D	E	F	G	H	I	J	K
M	M	N	O	P	Q	R	S	T	U	V	W	X	Y	Z	A	B	C	D	E	F	G	H	I	J	K	L
N	N	O	P	Q	R	S	T	U	V	W	X	Y	Z	A	B	C	D	E	F	G	H	I	J	K	L	M
O	O	P	Q	R	S	T	U	V	W	X	Y	Z	A	B	C	D	E	F	G	H	I	J	K	L	M	N
P	P	Q	R	S	T	U	V	W	X	Y	Z	A	B	C	D	E	F	G	H	I	J	K	L	M	N	O
Q	Q	R	S	T	U	V	W	X	Y	Z	A	B	C	D	E	F	G	H	I	J	K	L	M	N	O	P
R	R	S	T	U	V	W	X	Y	Z	A	B	C	D	E	F	G	H	I	J	K	L	M	N	O	P	Q
S	S	T	U	V	W	X	Y	Z	A	B	C	D	E	F	G	H	I	J	K	L	M	N	O	P	Q	R
T	T	U	V	W	X	Y	Z	A	B	C	D	E	F	G	H	I	J	K	L	M	N	O	P	Q	R	S
U	U	V	W	X	Y	Z	A	B	C	D	E	F	G	H	I	J	K	L	M	N	O	P	Q	R	S	T
V	V	W	X	Y	Z	A	B	C	D	E	F	G	H	I	J	K	L	M	N	O	P	Q	R	S	T	U
W	W	X	Y	Z	A	B	C	D	E	F	G	H	I	J	K	L	M	N	O	P	Q	R	S	T	U	V
X	X	Y	Z	A	B	C	D	E	F	G	H	I	J	K	L	M	N	O	P	Q	R	S	T	U	V	W
Y	Y	Z	B	B	C	D	E	F	G	H	I	J	K	L	M	N	O	P	Q	R	S	T	U	V	W	X
Z	Z	A	C	C	D	E	F	G	H	I	J	K	L	M	N	O	P	Q	R	S	T	U	V	W	X	Y

Vigenère Cipher Grid for practise work

	A	B	C	D	E	F	G	H	I	J	K	L	M	N	O	P	Q	R	S	T	U	V	W	X	Y	Z
A	A	B	C	D	E	F	G	H	I	J	K	L	M	N	O	P	Q	R	S	T	U	V	W	X	Y	Z
B	B	C	D	E	F	G	H	I	J	K	L	M	N	O	P	Q	R	S	T	U	V	W	X	Y	Z	A
C	C	D	E	F	G	H	I	J	K	L	M	N	O	P	Q	R	S	T	U	V	W	X	Y	Z	A	B
D	D	E	F	G	H	I	J	K	L	M	N	O	P	Q	R	S	T	U	V	W	X	Y	Z	A	B	C
E	E	F	G	H	I	J	K	L	M	N	O	P	Q	R	S	T	U	V	W	X	Y	Z	A	B	C	D
F	F	G	H	I	J	K	L	M	N	O	P	Q	R	S	T	U	V	W	X	Y	Z	A	B	C	D	E
G	G	H	I	J	K	L	M	N	O	P	Q	R	S	T	U	V	W	X	Y	Z	A	B	C	D	E	F
H	H	I	J	K	L	M	N	O	P	Q	R	S	T	U	V	W	X	Y	Z	A	B	C	D	E	F	G
I	I	J	K	L	M	N	O	P	Q	R	S	T	U	V	W	X	Y	Z	A	B	C	D	E	F	G	H
J	J	K	L	M	N	O	P	Q	R	S	T	U	V	W	X	Y	Z	A	B	C	D	E	F	G	H	I
K	K	L	M	N	O	P	Q	R	S	T	U	V	W	X	Y	Z	A	B	C	D	E	F	G	H	I	J
L	L	M	N	O	P	Q	R	S	T	U	V	W	X	Y	Z	A	B	C	D	E	F	G	H	I	J	K
M	M	N	O	P	Q	R	S	T	U	V	W	X	Y	Z	A	B	C	D	E	F	G	H	I	J	K	L
N	N	O	P	Q	R	S	T	U	V	W	X	Y	Z	A	B	C	D	E	F	G	H	I	J	K	L	M
O	O	P	Q	R	S	T	U	V	W	X	Y	Z	A	B	C	D	E	F	G	H	I	J	K	L	M	N
P	P	Q	R	S	T	U	V	W	X	Y	Z	A	B	C	D	E	F	G	H	I	J	K	L	M	N	O
Q	Q	R	S	T	U	V	W	X	Y	Z	A	B	C	D	E	F	G	H	I	J	K	L	M	N	O	P
R	R	S	T	U	V	W	X	Y	Z	A	B	C	D	E	F	G	H	I	J	K	L	M	N	O	P	Q
S	S	T	U	V	W	X	Y	Z	A	B	C	D	E	F	G	H	I	J	K	L	M	N	O	P	Q	R
T	T	U	V	W	X	Y	Z	A	B	C	D	E	F	G	H	I	J	K	L	M	N	O	P	Q	R	S
U	U	V	W	X	Y	Z	A	B	C	D	E	F	G	H	I	J	K	L	M	N	O	P	Q	R	S	T
V	V	W	X	Y	Z	A	B	C	D	E	F	G	H	I	J	K	L	M	N	O	P	Q	R	S	T	U
W	W	X	Y	Z	A	B	C	D	E	F	G	H	I	J	K	L	M	N	O	P	Q	R	S	T	U	V
X	X	Y	Z	A	B	C	D	E	F	G	H	I	J	K	L	M	N	O	P	Q	R	S	T	U	V	W
Y	Y	Z	B	B	C	D	E	F	G	H	I	J	K	L	M	N	O	P	Q	R	S	T	U	V	W	X
Z	Z	A	C	C	D	E	F	G	H	I	J	K	L	M	N	O	P	Q	R	S	T	U	V	W	X	Y

Printed in Great Britain
by Amazon

43457567R00056